Social Studies Learning Centers for the Primary Grades

Carol A. Poppe
and
Nancy A. Van Matre

Illustrated by Nancy A. Van Matre

THE CENTER FOR APPLIED
RESEARCH IN EDUCATION
West Nyack, New York 10995

Library of Congress Cataloging-in-Publication Data

Poppe, Carol A.
    Social studies learning centers for the primary grades / Carol A.
Poppe, and Nancy A. Van Matre ; illustrated by Nancy A. Van Matre.
        p.   cm.
    ISBN 0-87628-795-X

    1. Social sciences—Study and teaching (Primary)   2. Classroom
learning centers.   3. Activity programs in education.   I. Van Matre,
Nancy A.   II. Title
LB1530.P67   1989
372.83′044—dc20   89-7241
                                                         CIP

ISBN 0-87628-795-X

THE CENTER FOR APPLIED
RESEARCH IN EDUCATION
BUSINESS & PROFESSIONAL DIVISION
A division of Simon & Schuster
West Nyack, New York 10995

Printed in the United States of America

Dedication

For Michael and Jason who set a record for
love, patience, endurance, and fast food meals
as they survived the writing of Book 3.

About the Authors

CAROL A. POPPE received her B.A. degree from Ohio University and has taken several graduate courses at Oakland University and Siena Heights College. Mrs. Poppe has 24 years of teaching experience at the first- and second-grade levels.

NANCY A. VAN MATRE received her B.A. degree from Eastern Michigan University, and her M.A. degree in Reading. She has been actively teaching grades one through three for over 13 years.

Both authors have enjoyed writing together since 1982 and are the coauthors of *Science Learning Centers for the Primary Grades* (The Center for Applied Research in Education, 1985) and *K-3 Science Activities Kit* (The Center for Applied Research in Education, 1988). They have presented several learning center workshops for other educators and are currently teaching first grade in the Clinton Community Schools in Clinton, Michigan. Learning center activities, like the ones in this book, have been an integral part of their daily classroom schedules since 1976.

About This Book

Social Studies Learning Centers for the Primary Grades is designed to help the primary teacher develop and manage a system in which each child participates daily at an individual social studies learning center. Specifically, it presents five ready-to-use social studies learning center units based on particular themes, along with proven techniques for using learning centers as an integral part of the classroom routine.

The five social studies units are:

1. **ABOUT ME:** activities develop children's awareness that each person is unique
2. **FAMILY:** activities focus on the family as a special kind of group
3. **SCHOOL:** activities emphasize the school environment and school workers
4. **COMMUNITY:** activities promote children's understanding of the local community and its people
5. **STATE:** activities feature comparisons of physical characteristics, symbols, and products

Each learning center unit includes eight ready-to-use file folder activities that reinforce basic social studies skills as well as communication, math, and motor skills. A complete listing of the skills taught and reinforced in each area is shown in the accompanying table. And each of the 40 learning center activities provides complete directions for its successful use along with reproducible student pages. For each activity you will find:

- content areas covered by the activity
- specific skills required to do the activity
- materials needed to complete the activity
- easy-to-follow preparation procedures
- reproducible student direction and activity pages
- critical thinking skill questions
- one-step-beyond enrichment activities

Social Studies Learning Center Units	Social Studies					Communication						Math			Motor				
	Mapping	Classifying	Comparing	Using References	Self-Image	Critical Thinking	Summarizing	Creative Writing	Listening	Spelling	Vocabulary Development	Measurement	Problem Solving	Sorting	Art/Creating	Coordination	Handwriting	Sort/Matching	Teacher's Choice
About Me	x	x	x	x	x	x	x	x	x	x		x			x	x	x	x	x
Family	x	x	x	x	x	x	x	x	x		x	x		x	x	x	x	x	x
School	x	x	x	x	x	x	x	x	x		x	x			x	x	x	x	x
Community	x	x	x	x	x	x	x	x	x	x	x		x	x	x	x	x	x	x
State	x	x	x	x	x	x	x	x	x	x	x	x	x		x	x	x	x	x

In addition to the individual activities which students can complete on their own, each unit also presents a wide assortment of small- and large-group experiences, innovative home research projects with parental involvement and feedback, maps, letters, awards, and summary pages.

These social studies learning center units offer a practical and stimulating way to enhance children's self-concept, encourage independent exploration and learning, develop thinking skills, and promote cooperation among all members of the class. They also foster parent involvement with their child's learning and promote communication among parent, child, and teacher.

The last section of *Social Studies Learning Centers for the Primary Grades* describes a rotating management system for using the learning center activities as part of your daily classroom routine. Included is a Color Wheel technique for controlling each child's movement among four different classroom work areas: learning centers, reading, seatwork, and boardwork. Using this system, every child has a chance to complete all eight activities in a given learning center unit over an eight-day period.

The ideas and activities presented here will be useful to resource-room teachers and teachers of special education as well as primary classroom teachers. The units are appropriate for students in kindergarten through third grade, and are useful for students at all developmental levels. Each set of directions for the social studies learning centers combines illustrations with simple sentences to enable virtually every child to complete the activities independently.

As educators, we are life touchers. We have a role in nurturing lives. We hope you will enjoy using these activities to bring out the uniqueness of each student whose life you touch.

Carol A. Poppe
Nancy A. Van Matre

To the Teacher

Constructing the Social Studies Learning Center File Folders:

The directions for each of the Social Studies Activities in this book are designed to fit on 12″ × 18″ file folders. Bright colored file folders are attractive for this purpose. A glue stick works well for mounting the direction pages. Crayons or water based marking pens may be used to color the pictures and numbers. (Prior to mounting any directions, be sure the other side of the page has been duplicated for future use).

How to make the direction file folder:

1. Glue the "Teacher Directions" to the back of the file folder. (This visual aid is helpful to the teacher in organizing the necessary materials for the Social Studies activity.)
2. Glue the "Directions for File Folder Activities" to the adjacent back side of the file folder.

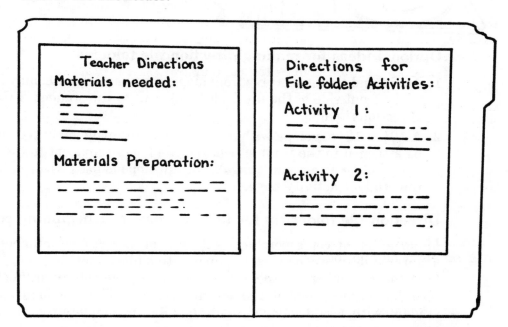

3. Color the pictures on the student "File Folder Directions" page.
4. Color the numbers orange on the student "File Folder Directions" page. (Use the same format for all of the file folders.)
5. Glue the student "File Folder Directions" page to the front of the file folder.
6. Laminate or use clear self-stick vinyl to cover all of the direction file folders.

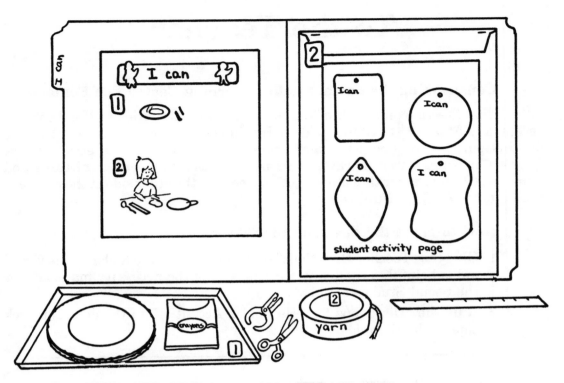

Optional ideas for making direction file folders:

1. Additional theme pictures from magazines, catalogs, etc. may be glued to the front side of the file folder (adjacent to the student "File Folder Directions" page).

2. A 10″ × 13″ envelope with a student activity page mounted on it may be attached to the front side of the file folder (adjacent to the student "File Folder Directions" page). The envelope is used as a container for the student activity page.

Direction file folder tip for the non-reader or beginning reader:

Make a set of corresponding "File Folder Directions" numbers on 1″ squares of orange construction paper with a black marking pen. Staple or tape these numbers to the student activity page container, books, tape recorder, games, etc. at the learning center. The numbers assist the student with less developed reading skills to complete the activities in sequential order.

Social Studies Activities Preparation:

The amount of student input will vary depending on your students' ages.
As you begin a new Social Studies unit you may wish to refer to the discussion questions in the "Thinking It Over" section to evaluate your student's background knowledge. You may wish to add or delete ideas to meet the specific

needs of your group. Encourage student input regarding the specific information they may wish to learn about.

The students may be able to create their own "One Step Beyond Activities."

You may wish to involve students in the preparation of materials for the Social Studies unit activities. You will need to refer to the "Materials needed" and the "Materials preparation" sections of the "Teacher's Directions" to plan the student's tasks.

A few days prior to beginning a new Social Studies unit, divide the students into small groups. Assign each group various jobs such as designing bulletin boards, coloring direction file folders, making patterns, and preparing cassette tapes.

Storing the Social Studies Units:

It is helpful to keep the direction file folders and materials for each Social Studies Unit in a large cardboard storage box. An ideal size is 24″ × 16″ × 12″ high with a lid (most discount stores have these boxes in flat packages). The same size boxes can be easily labeled, carried, and stacked utilizing a minimum amount of floor space. The master social studies activities list may be taped inside the lid for easy reference.

Contents

School • 90

Community • 134

State • 177

LEARNING CENTER MANAGEMENT • 225

SOCIAL STUDIES LEARNING CENTER UNITS

About Me

Draw yourself in the mirror.

Center Marker

"ABOUT ME" CENTER MARKER

A learning center marker is provided for students using the Social Studies unit at learning centers. (Refer to page 230.)

Distribute copies of the mirror marker to the students. The students can draw their faces on the mirror markers, cut out their markers, and place them near the "About Me" Learning Centers.

ABOUT ME

Date _____

Dear Parent,
    The theme of our next social studies unit will be "About Me." Your child will develop a better understanding of his or her feelings, growth, abilities, similarities, differences, and surroundings.
    I will need a recent photograph of your child approximately _____ size for our "Look at Me" learning center. Label the picture on the back with your child's name. The photograph will be returned at the end of the school year.
    Thank you for encouraging your child to make a living room map. At the "My Home" area he or she will do additional map activities. Your child will sort and tack furniture cards onto appropriate rooms of the home bulletin board map. He or she will complete a student activity page.
    Anticipate receiving a long growth chart. Please help your child display it. Encourage your child to measure and record his or her height every six months.
    Please send the photograph, living room map, and the following "Growth Chart Information" by _____.
    Thank you for your continued support. You are welcome to stop in and see our "About Me" learning centers.

Sincerely,

Your child's teacher

Growth Chart Information

_____
child's name

_____
length at birth

_____
birth date: *month*   *day*   *year*

Date _____ ,

From Home
To School

Dear _____ ,

_____
_____
_____
_____
_____
_____
_____
_____
_____
_____
_____
_____
_____
_____
_____
_____

_____
Parent Signature

Dear Parent,

    I would appreciate any feedback you or your child may have regarding the "About Me" Social Studies activities: My Home, I Am Special, My Name, When I Grow Up, My Feelings, Look At Me, I Can, and How I've Grown.

    Please use this page for comments and return it to me by _____ .

Sincerely,

Your child's teacher

"ABOUT ME" LEARNING CENTERS LIST

These activities emphasize self-concept.

"My Home" Center

(Bulletin board is used with this activity.)
Content area: Social Studies
Skills: Sorting, Classifying, Map
Activities:

1. Sort and tack the furniture cards onto the home.
2. Color, cut, sort, and paste furniture on the student activity page.

"I Am Special" Center

Content area: Motor and Social Studies
Skills: Fine-Motor Coordination, Creating, Self-Image
Activities:

1. Trace poster pattern.
2. Write special things about yourself on poster.

"My Name" Center

Content area: Motor and Communication
Skills: Sorting, Ordering, Spelling, Fine-Motor Coordination
Activities:

1. Spell your name on the flannelboard.
2. Cut out the letters in your name from a magazine.
3. Paste letters in order to spell your name.

"When I Grow Up" Center

Content area: Communication and Motor

Skills: Creative Writing, Creating, Using References

Activities:

1. Paint a picture depicting yourself as a grown-up.
2. Write a story, "When I Grow Up I Will Be . . ."

"My Feelings" Center (Open-ended activity)

Content area: Communication, Motor, and Teacher's Choice

Skills: Listening, Fine-Motor Coordination, Teacher's Choice

Activities:

1. Listen to cassette tape of the book.
2. Make a matching game.

"Look at Me" Center

Content area: Social Studies, Communication, and Motor

Skills: Fine-Motor, Comparing, Classifying

Activities:

1. Make a same and different book.
2. Copy mirror cards and record information.

"I Can" Center

Content area: Math, Motor, Social Studies

Skills: Measuring (Linear), Creating, Self-Image

Activities:

1. Draw your face on a paper plate.
2. Make a mobile.

"How I've Grown" Center

Content area: Math

Skills: Measuring (Linear)

Activities:

1. Make your growth chart.
2. Measure yourself and record measurements on chart.

TEACHER'S DIRECTIONS FOR "MY HOME" CENTER

Content area: Social Studies

Skills: Sorting, classifying, map

Materials needed:

> Bulletin board
> Copies of student activity page
> Furniture cards and container
> Thumbtacks and container
> Crayons
> Pencil
> Scissors
> Paste

Materials preparation:

You or the students:

- Make the "My Home" bulletin board map as pictured on the file folder directions page.
- Prepare a set of furniture picture cards for the bulletin board (at least four per room). Cut and paste a variety of magazine or catalog pictures on 3″ × 5″ index cards such as the pictures on the student activity page.

Optional activity: you may provide a doll house with furniture for the students to sort into the appropriate rooms.

Activity 1

The student sorts and tacks the furniture cards onto the home on the bulletin board.

Activity 2

The student colors, cuts, sorts, and pastes the furniture into the appropriate rooms on the student activity page.

Optional activities:

The older student may write the names of the furniture on the student activity page using references.
The student may sort furniture into the appropriate rooms of a doll house.

Thinking it over:

Discussion questions:

1. How long have you lived in your home?
2. Did you buy your home from another owner?
3. Did you have a new home built for you?
   What kinds of workers helped build your home?
   What tools did they use?
   Did someone have blueprints? (If so, encourage the student to share them.)
4. How many people live in your home?
5. Do you have pets living inside your home?
6. How many rooms are in your home?
7. Where do you go inside your home if you want to be alone?

One step beyond activities:

1. The student may design a dream room which may be added to his or her home. The room could be drawn on paper; constructed with discarded materials, such as cardboard tubes, construction paper scraps, yarn, and so on; or made inside a shoebox like a diorama.
2. The student could write a story or tell about the room. Some ideas are: "What would you like to have in your room?" "What would you like to do in the room?" "Who could use the room?"
3. The student could write a story about his or her home.
4. Encourage the students to bring in blueprints or provide a set for them. The students could draw a room on graph paper.

My Home

1

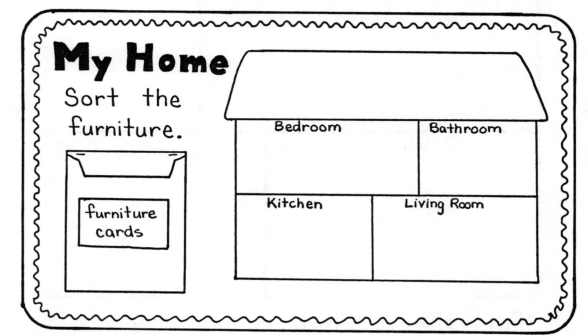

My Home

Sort the furniture.

furniture cards

Bedroom	Bathroom
Kitchen	Living Room

2 Do the ditto.

File Folder Directions

Bedroom	Bathroom
Kitchen	Living Room

Put the furniture in the rooms. name _____

Student Activity Page

TEACHER'S DIRECTIONS FOR THE "I AM SPECIAL" CENTER

Content areas: Social studies and motor

Skills: Self-image, creating, fine-motor coordination

Materials needed:

> Large pieces of paper
> Pencil
> An assortment of fine-line permanent marking pens
> Poster pattern

Materials preparation:

You or the students:

 • Make a poster pattern similar to the one pictured on the file folder directions page.

You may wish to write an appropriate number of sentence starters on the pattern for younger students and laminate it. Some ideas are:

> I like to eat _____.
> I like to play with _____.
> I have a _____ for a pet.
> I can do _____ by myself.
> I like to play _____ best on the playground.

DIRECTIONS FOR FILE FOLDER ACTIVITIES:

Activity 1

The student traces the pattern on large paper to make a poster.

Activity 2

The student uses marking pens to write "_____ is Special," and additional information about him or herself on the poster. The younger student may refer to the teacher-made pattern. He or she draws eyes, mouth, hair, and so on to complete the poster.

Thinking it over:

Discussion questions:

1. What makes you feel important?
2. What has someone said to you to make you feel special?
3. Do you have a job at home? Who gave you the job? Why?
4. What do you do best in Gym?
5. What do you do best in the classroom?
6. Did you ever win a prize? How did you feel?
7. How can you show you think somebody is special?

One step beyond activities:

1. Each child can make an "I am Special" bag or box at home. He or she can put a collection of things in it that are about him or her. Some ideas are: photographs of pets, special events, trip souvenirs, favorite toys, original pictures, stories, or poems, prizes, and so on. Arrange times for the students to share their boxes. You may wish to schedule this activity over a multiday span with a few students participating each day.
2. Read books such as Berry, Joy, *Every Kid's Guide to Being Special,* Childrens Press, Chicago, 1987; Greene, Laura, *I Am Somebody,* Childrens Press, Chicago, 1980; and discuss them. The students can draw pictures about the books.

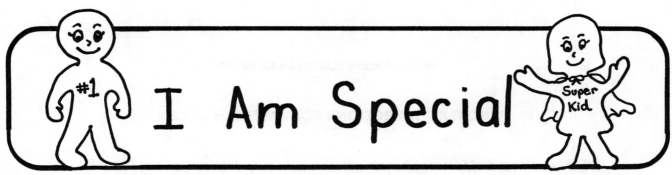

I Am Special

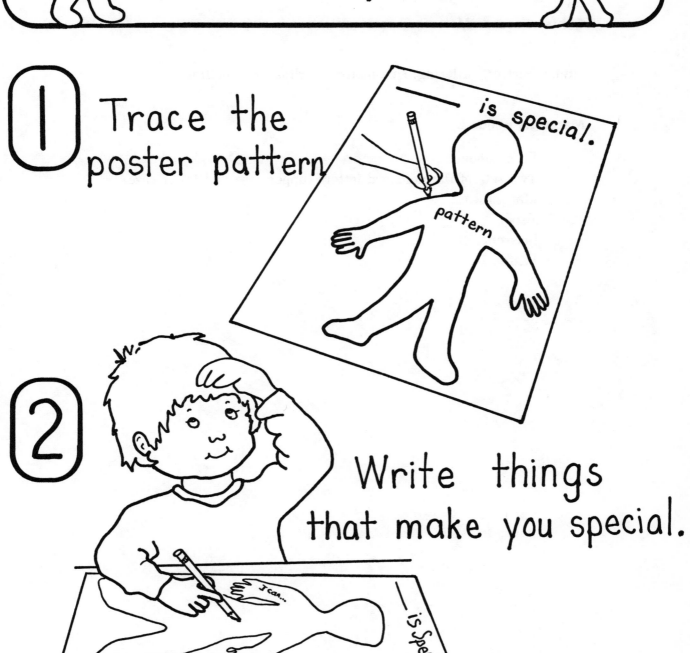

1 Trace the poster pattern

is special.

pattern

2 Write things that make you special.

I can...

is Special

File Folder Directions

TEACHER'S DIRECTIONS FOR "MY NAME" CENTER

Content areas: Motor and communication

Skills: Sorting, ordering, fine-motor coordination, spelling

Materials needed:

> Flannelboard
> Two sets of flannelboard letters (upper case and lower case)
> Magazines
> Paper
> Scissors
> Paste

DIRECTIONS FOR FILE FOLDER ACTIVITIES:

Activity 1

The student uses the upper case and lower case letters to spell his or her name on the flannelboard.

Activity 2

The student cuts out the letters in his or her name from a magazine. He or she pastes the letters in order to spell his or her name.

Thinking it over:

Discussion questions:

1. Who named you?
2. When were you named?
3. Were you named for someone in your family?
4. Do you have a nickname?
5. Do you like your name?
6. If you could change your name, what name would you choose?

One step beyond activities:

1. Make a "Guess Who?" book. Each student cuts out the letters of his or her first name out of wallpaper. He or she pastes the letters in mixed order on a 12″ × 18″ piece of construction paper. The name pages are compiled into a class book. The students guess who designed each page.
2. The student makes a list of the names of the people in his or her family. He or she arranges the first names in alphabetical order.
3. Make a large chart that shows the etymology of each of your student's names. Provide name references, such as baby name derivation books. The students look up and write the meaning of their names.
4. The student writes his or her name vertically on a piece of paper. Then he or she writes a word beginning with each letter in the name that will describe him or her.

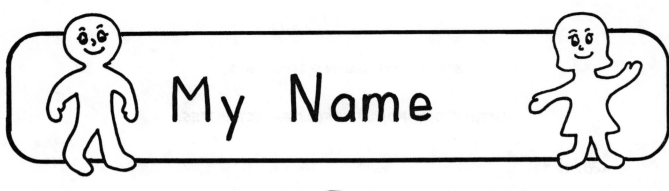

My Name

1

Spell your name on the flannel board.

2 Find all the letters in your name. Cut and paste them in order.

File Folder Directions

TEACHER'S DIRECTIONS FOR "WHEN I GROW UP" CENTER

Content areas: Communication and motor

Skills: Creative writing, creating, using references

Materials needed:

Easel
Paint
Paintbrushes
Paper
Handwriting paper
Pencil
References: pictionary, dictionary, career books

DIRECTIONS FOR FILE FOLDER ACTIVITIES:

Activity 1

The student paints a picture depicting himself or herself when he or she is grown-up.

Activity 2

He or she writes a story: "When I grow up, I will be . . .," using available references.

Thinking it over:

Discussion questions:

1. What kinds of things would you do on your job?
2. What would you wear?
3. Would you need tools? What kind?
4. What time would you go to work? Return?
5. How would you get to work?
6. What would you like about your job? Dislike?
7. How much money would you make?
8. Would you need to go to college to get training for your job? Why or why not?
9. Will you help people in your job? If so, how?

One step beyond activities:

1. The student can list the kinds of jobs that would require him or her to go to school to learn.
2. The student can list the kinds of jobs that would provide on-site training.
3. The student can taperecord a story about the person he or she would like to be.
4. The student can write about the hobbies or interests he or she might look forward to doing in his or her leisure time.

When I Grow Up

1

What could you be when you grow up? Paint it.

2

Write a story: "When I grow up I will be___."

File Folder Directions

TEACHER'S DIRECTIONS FOR "MY FEELINGS" CENTER

(Open-ended activity)

Content areas: Communication, motor, and teacher's choice

Skills: Listening, fine-motor coordination, teacher's choice

Materials needed:

> Tape recorder
> Cassette tape
> Pencil
> Crayons
> Scissors
> A lid or circular piece of posterboard (approximately 3″ diameter)
> One 12″ by 18″ piece of paper per student
> A book about feelings such as Berry, Joy, *Every Kid's Guide to Handling Feelings,* Childrens Press, Chicago, 1987; Blume, Judy, *The One in the Middle is the Green Kangaroo,* Dell Publishing Co., New York, 1981; Conta, Marcia, and Reardon, Maureen, *Feelings Between Friends,* Advanced Concepts, Inc., Milwaukee, 1974, Viorst, Judith, *Alexander and the Terrible, Horrible, No Good, Very Bad Day,* MacMillan Publishing Co., New York, 1972.
> Teacher-made reference chart

Materials preparation:

- Prepare a cassette tape of the book.
- Make a reference chart:
  Trace around a circular pattern 8 times on 12″ by 18″ paper (2 rows of 4 each). Make a matching game to reinforce or review a skill. Some ideas are: Math problems, opposite words, and so on. Write a different word on each circle in the top row. Write a matching word on each circle in the bottom row (such as "happy" in the top row and "sad" in the bottom row). Cut out the circles and laminate them. Provide a container for the game. **Optional:** the older student may make 16 or more circles.

DIRECTIONS FOR FILE FOLDER ACTIVITIES:

Activity 1

The student listens to the cassette tape of the book.

Activity 2

The student makes a matching game referring to the teacher-made reference chart. He or she turns over each pair of matching circles and draws matching faces depicting feelings on the opposite sides, thus making the game self-checking.

Thinking it over:

Discussion questions:

1. Is it okay to have different kinds of feelings?
2. How can feelings change?
3. How would you feel if someone laughed when you tried something that did not work?
4. What would you say if a friend showed you a trick that he or she could do?
5. How did you feel when you learned to tie your shoes?
6. How would you feel if your dog dug up your neighbor's garden?

One step beyond activities:

1. *Feelings Charades:* Encourage the students to think of a variety of feelings. You or the students write these feelings on 3″ by 5″ index cards. Each student can draw a card and act out the emotion for the class to guess.
2. The students can do creative writing about feelings. Some ideas are:
   "I get scared when _____."
   "One day I was really embarrassed when _____."
   "I feel happiest when _____."
   "Boy, do I ever get angry when _____."

 # My Feelings

1 Listen to the book about feelings.

2 Make a matching game.

Trace a lid.
Write on circles.
Cut out circles.

File Folder Directions

TEACHER'S DIRECTIONS FOR "LOOK AT ME" CENTER

Content area: Social studies, communication, and motor

Skills: Fine-motor coordination, comparing, classifying

Materials needed:

> Copies of student activity page
> Attribute cards and container
> Mirror
> Pencil
> Crayons
> Stapler/staples
> Photograph or drawing of each student

Materials preparation:

- Provide a mirror at this center for students to use in distinguishing similarities and differences.
- You or the students make a picture display:
  > Mount student photographs, which were requested in the parent letter, on construction paper. Write student's first/last names and birthdate on the construction paper with a dark permanent marking pen. (**Optional:** students may draw pictures of their heads. Stress using mirror for correct eye and hair color.) Put pictures on a bulletin board, wall, etc. at the center area.
  >
  > You or the students make a set of attribute cards. You may wish to use the mirror Center Marker for a pattern. Write one idea on each card. Some ideas are: eye color, hair color, birth month, first name, first letter of last name, and so on.
  >
  > You will need to determine the number of student activity pages in each book (older student may do several). You will also need to decide on a way to assemble the book, such as stapling.

DIRECTIONS FOR FILE FOLDER ACTIVITIES:

Activity 1

The student makes a book using copies of the student activity page.

Activity 2

The student copies the attribute cards on each page, such as eye color. He or she refers to the picture display to find three students who have the same eye color as his or hers. Then he or she finds three students that have different eye colors. The student records the names on the pages in his or her book.

Thinking it over:

Discussion questions:

1. How many students have first names that start with "J"?
2. What children have freckles?
3. How many boys have brown hair?
4. How many girls have one or more teeth missing?
5. How many girls have black hair?
6. Who is the tallest person in our class?
7. Who has the shortest hair in our class?
8. Can you think of other ways that some of us are alike?
9. Can you think of other ways that some of us are different?

One step beyond activities:

1. Attribute game: The students sit in a circle. Each person takes a turn in the middle. He or she chooses another child who has a similar attribute. The other students guess what attribute is similar. (Vary the game for likenesses and differences.)
2. "Who Am I?" game: (Prior to playing the game, make it clear that only "friendly descriptions" may be given. Stress that nobody would enjoy playing a game that embarrasses or makes you feel uncomfortable.) The students sit in a circle. One person is IT. He or she describes any characteristics of another child in the group. For example, Bill might describe himself as Mary by saying, "I'm a girl with blonde hair and green eyes. I have on a red dress. Who am I?"
3. You may want to make a graph of student attributes, such as eye colors, hair colors, missing teeth, freckles, and so on.

Look At Me

1

Make your book.

2 Copy words onto each page. Write names.

File Folder Directions

Student Activity Page

TEACHER'S DIRECTIONS FOR THE "I CAN" CENTER

Content areas: Math, motor, and social studies

Skills: Measuring (linear), creating, self-image

Materials needed:

> Copies of student activity page
> One paper plate (9″ diameter) per student
> One 5′ piece of yarn, string, or wire per student
> Paper puncher
> Ruler
> Scissors
> Crayons
> References: dictionary, pictionary

Materials preparation:

- You may want to have a class discussion emphasizing many different things that the students can do, such as ride bikes, tie shoes, bake cakes, or make beds, prior to beginning this activity. (Note that no one child should be expected to know how to do them all.)
- You may want to make a paper plate pattern like the one pictured on the File Folder Directions page.

DIRECTIONS FOR FILE FOLDER ACTIVITIES:

Activity 1

The student draws his or her face on a paper plate. Then he or she punches five holes around the outer edge of the plate with a paper puncher.

Activity 2

1. The student cuts out the shapes on the student activity page. He or she punches a hole in each dot with a paper puncher.
2. He or she completes the sentences ("I Can . . .") on the front of each shape using references.
3. The student illustrates the sentence on the back of each shape.
4. He or she measures and cuts the yarn into 5 pieces (12").
5. The student ties one end of each piece of yarn through a hole in the shape. He or she ties the opposite end of the yarn to a hole in the plate.
6. The student may put the remaining piece of yarn through the top hole of the plate and tie it to form a loop hanger.

Thinking it over:

Discussion questions:

1. What things have you learned to do at school this year?
2. What things have you learned to do at home this year?
3. How did you feel when you accomplished new things?
4. What can you do now that you couldn't do when you were a three-year-old?
5. Can you predict some things you might be able to do in two years? Ten years? Twenty years?

One step beyond activities:

1. Play follow-the-leader games to help the students identify things they can and cannot do. You may want to include physical skills such as crawling, running, hopping, skipping, and so on. (As a follow-up activity, you may want to pair students to practice improving their skills.)
2. Play cumulative games such as "Going to the Mall" to get objects. A player must remember and recite all objects previously mentioned before adding his or her own objects.
3. Make a class chart listing one thing that each child can do. Encourage thinking about things the students can do with their bodies, minds, senses, as well as socially and emotionally.
4. Encourage each child to make a list of things he or she is learning now and things he or she wants to learn. The student may want to record his or her accomplishments for one or more months on a calendar, in a journal, or an "I Can" book.

I Can

1 Make your face.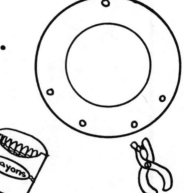

Punch holes around the edge.

2 Make the shapes.

Tie them to the face.

File Folder Directions

Things I can do

I can

I can

I can

I can

Student Activity Page

TEACHER'S DIRECTIONS FOR "HOW I'VE GROWN" CENTER

Content area: Math

Skills: Measuring (linear)

Materials needed:

> Copies of student activity page
> Ruler or tape measure
> Glue
> Crayons
> Pencil
> Paper (wall paper, shelf paper, chart paper, and so on) approximately 8½″ wide
> Two paper clips per student
> Tape

Materials preparation:

- You or the students cut strips of paper: one strip per student. Cut the paper 12″ longer than the height of the tallest student in the class. It will be helpful to roll, paper clip, and stand the paper in a box at the center area.
- You will need to provide a container with the growth information slips requested in the parent letter.

DIRECTIONS FOR FILE FOLDER ACTIVITIES:

Activity 1

The student glues the student activity page growth chart onto the bottom of the roll of paper. He or she tapes the roll of paper to a wall making sure that the bottom edge of the chart is touching the floor.

Activity 2

The student measures himself or herself. (He or she may prefer to have another student help him or her.) He or she marks his or her current height on the chart with a red crayon. He or she marks his or her birth length with a green crayon. He or she writes the information on his or her chart and colors the pictures.

Thinking it over:

Discussion questions:

1. How can you tell you have grown from September to the following September?
2. Do you have any of the clothes you wore when you were a baby?
3. In what ways have you grown since you were a baby? What caused the changes in your growth?
4. In what ways do other animals change?
5. In what ways do plants grow?

One step beyond activities:

1. Record the students' lengths at birth and current heights on a chart or graph. Compare the lengths: Were the tallest students also the longest babies?
2. Encourage the students to bring in baby pictures with their names on the back. Display the pictures on a "Who's Looking at You?" bulletin board. After a few days let the students take turns identifying the babies. You may want to include your picture also.
3. Arrange to have your students' siblings visit the class. Compare likenesses and differences within families.
4. You may want to schedule a visit with another class in your school to emphasize the growth changes.

How I've Grown

1 Make your growth chart.

2 Measure yourself.

Fill in the blanks.

File Folder Directions

_____'s Growth Chart

Today is _____.
I am ____ years old.
Today I'm _____ tall.
On the day I was
born, _____ 19___,
I was ____ long.
I have grown ____ since then.
In 6 months I will find out
how much I've grown.

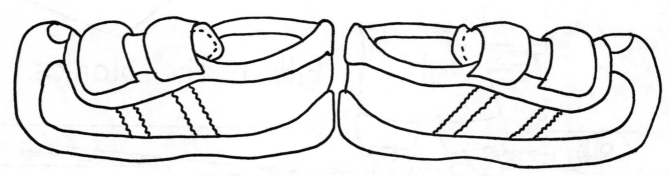

Student Activity Page

TEACHER'S SUGGESTIONS FOR "ABOUT ME" ENRICHMENT ACTIVITIES

"About Me" group activity

Living Room Books, "Appreciation Day," "Come-As-What-You-Want-To-Be Party"

"About Me" home activity

Duplicate the pages on colored paper. Send the pages home two weeks prior to beginning the "About Me" social studies unit. Encourage the students to draw the living room maps.

"About Me" awards

Duplicate the pages on colored paper. Give each child who returns the "About Me" Home Activity map a Home Activity Award. The other "About Me" Awards may be used for the recognition of good work, and so on.

"About Me" summary activity

Duplicate "I'm special because . . ." summary page. Discuss and review the "About Me" completed activities prior to giving the students the "I'm special because . . ." page. Encourage the student to complete the page by drawing his or her features in the head outline, writing adjectives or phrases describing his or her unique characteristics in the balloons, and coloring the illustrations.

"ABOUT ME" GROUP ACTIVITIES

The following are suggestions for culminating activities for the "About Me" Social Studies unit:

1. *A class living room book*

When the living room maps are returned, give the students an opportunity to share them. You may want to have students discuss likenesses and differences of rooms. The student can write an experience story or write about his or her living room. Some ideas are: "In my living room, I like to . . . ," "A funny thing happened when I was alone in my living room," "If I could re-decorate my living room, I would . . ." Compile the maps and stories in a class book.

2. *"Appreciation day"*

At the beginning of the school day each student writes his or her name on a piece of paper and puts it into a box. Then each student draws one name out of the box. He or she makes a card, writes a poem, writes a story, designs a poster, and so on to show appreciation of the person. He or she could put the gift into a bag or construction paper envelope decorated with the person's favorite colors, toys, pets, and so on. Arrange a time later in the day for the students to exchange their gifts.

3. *"Come-as-what-you-want-to-be-party"*

Plan a party with the students furnishing light refreshments. The students could design placemats with picture or word riddles about the persons they wished to be when they grow up. Encourage each student to bring a costume depicting himself or herself in a grown-up capacity. The students would wear the costumes at the party. Each student could have a turn to share his or her riddle and costume; then other students could guess who he or she was depicting.

"ABOUT ME" HOME ACTIVITY
ENRICHMENT PAGE

Return by _____

Date _____

Dear Parent,

    In two weeks our class will begin an "About Me" Social Studies unit emphasizing self-concept. Students will be encouraged to become more aware of themselves and their surroundings.

    Please help your child draw a map of his or her living room on the attached map page. The purpose of this map activity is to: 1. help your child become more aware of his home environment; 2. understand that a map is a drawing of an area; 3. introduce the four cardinal directions: North, West, South, East; 4. use a number key for furniture symbols.

    On _____ your child will write a story about his or her living room referring to the map.

    As a group activity, the students will share their maps and stories. The maps and stories will be compiled into a class book.

    I appreciate your help with this map activity. We hope you will take the opportunity to read our map book when it is finished.

Sincerely,

Your child's teacher

name _____

return to school on _____

Draw a map of your livingroom.
Show the windows, doors and closet.
Use the number key for the furniture.

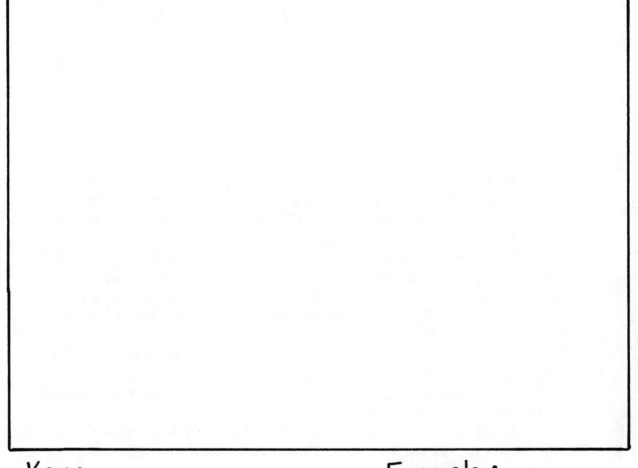

Key :

1. couch	6. T. V.
2. table	7. desk
3. chair	8. bookcase
4. chest	9. _____
5. lamp	10. _____

Example :

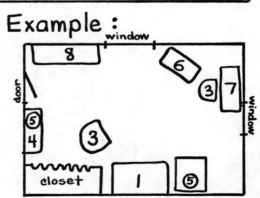

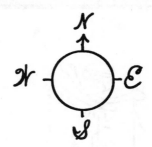

_____

North, South, East, or West
I am glad you did your best!

_____

Home Activity Award

How am I doing?
Better and better!

_____

_____

_____

"About Me" Award

You are a winner!

You can _____

_____

_____

_____

U.R.S.

(You are special!)

_____

_____

_____

_____

"About Me" Awards

About Me

I'm Special

because...

Draw what makes you special.

Summary Page

Family

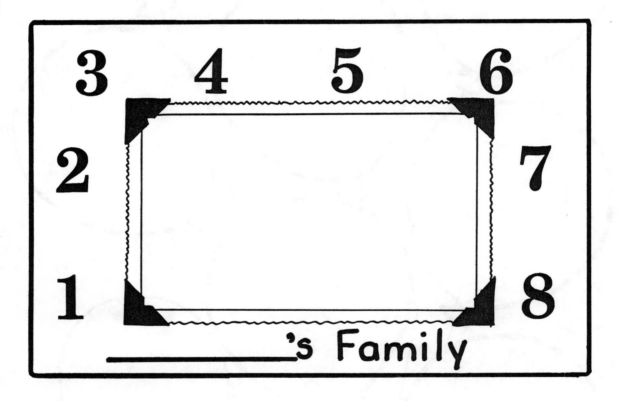

Draw your family in the picture.

Center Marker

"FAMILY" CENTER MARKER

A learning center marker is provided for students using the Social Studies unit at learning centers. (Refer to page 230.)

Distribute copies of the family markers to the students. The students may draw the family he or she resides with in the picture on the marker. The student may color the picture frame. The student can cut out the marker and place it near the "Family" Learning Centers.

GETTING TO KNOW YOU

Date _____

Dear Parent,

We will begin a Social Studies unit about families next week. We will learn about family wants, needs, recreation, birthdays, responsibilities, and so on.

A map of our school district with a drawing of each child's home will be featured on our bulletin board. Map skill activities emphasizing addresses will help your child develop an awareness of his home location in terms of streets.

At our Family Jobs center your child will list the ways he or she helps at home. Your child will make placemats for your dinner table. Please encourage your child to set the table.

Your child will write and mail a letter to a favorite relative. Please print the name and address of the relative on paper and send it to school inside an unsealed stamped envelope.

At the Family Tree center, your child will draw a large tree with pictures, names, birthdates, and birth places of family members you choose to include. You may wish to extend this activity at home.

Please fill out the attached "My Family Tree" information sheet and return it with the stamped envelope by _____.

Thank you for your continued support.

Sincerely,

Your child's teacher

"MY FAMILY TREE" INFORMATION SHEET

Please print the information for the members you wish to include.

	NAME	BIRTHDATE	BIRTH PLACE
Your child			
Father			
Mother			
Sisters			
Brothers			
Grandmothers			
Grandfathers			
Others			

Please return by _____

Date _____

Dear _____,

_____
_____
_____
_____
_____
_____
_____
_____
_____
_____
_____
_____
_____
_____

_____
Parent Signature

© 1989 by The Center for Applied Research in Education

Dear Parent,

   I would appreciate any feedback you or your child may have regarding the "Family" Social Studies activities: Where We Live, My Family Tree, Family Birthdays, Wants and Needs, Family Fun, Inside My House, Family Jobs, and My Favorite Relative.

   Please use this page for comments and return it to me by _____.

Sincerely,

Your child's teacher

"FAMILY" LEARNING CENTERS LIST

These activities focus on family characteristics and environment.

"Where We Live" Center

(A bulletin board is used with this center.)

Content areas: Social studies, math, motor

Skills: Mapping, comparing, sorting, handwriting

Activities:

1. Match house numbers on the map.
2. Make an address book.

"My Family Tree" Center

Content areas: Social studies, motor

Skills: Classifying, self-image, coordination

Activities:

1. Draw a tree.
2. Make pictures of family members.

"Family Birthdays" Center

Content areas: Math, motor

Skills: Time (months, ordinal numbers, coordination, matching)

Activities:

1. Play the birthday candle game.
2. Make your own game.
3. Make the envelope.

"Wants and Needs" Center

Content areas: Social studies, motor

Skills: Classifying, comparing, coordination

Activities:

1. Complete the student activity page by cutting, sorting, and pasting pictures of family needs.
2. Cut and paste magazine pictures of family wants onto a bag.

"Family Fun" Center

Content area: Social studies, communication, motor

Skills: Using reference materials, creative writing, creating

Activities:

1. Write a story, "My Family Has Fun."
2. Paint a picture about the story.

"Inside My House" Center

(Open-ended activity)

Content area: Communication, teacher's choice

Skills: Listening, vocabulary development, teacher's choice

Activities:

1. Listen to the book about houses.
2. Play matching game.
3. Complete house student activity page.

"Family Jobs" Center

Content area: Social studies, motor

Skills: Self-image, creating, sort-matching

Activities:

1. Complete "Ways I Help" paper.
2. Make placemats and set table.

"My Favorite Relative" Center

Content area: Communication, motor

Skills: Letter writing, handwriting

Activities:

1. Write a letter to a favorite relative.
2. Address the envelope.

TEACHER'S DIRECTIONS FOR "WHERE WE LIVE" CENTER

Content areas: Social studies, math, motor

Skills: Mapping, comparing, sorting, handwriting

Materials needed:

> Bulletin board
> Map of school district
> Teacher-made set of house number cards and container
> Teacher-made address book
> Paper: wallpaper, notebook, handwriting, newsprint, construction
> Pencil
> Stapler—staples
> Thumbtacks and container

Materials preparation:

- Prior to beginning Family learning centers each student draws and cuts out his or her house on a 3″ × 3″ piece of construction paper (use four different colors for the class). Write the students' names and house numbers on the houses with a marking pen.
- Make a matching set of house number cards out of the same colors of construction paper and laminate them.
- Prepare a map of your school district on the bulletin board. Staple the students' houses onto the proper map locations.
- Make an example address book. You will need to determine the number of pages, type of paper for cover and content pages, and the way to assemble the book. Write _____'s Address Book on the cover.

DIRECTIONS FOR FILE FOLDER ACTIVITIES:

Activity 1

The student tacks the house number cards onto the matching houses on the map.

Activity 2

The student makes an address book as per your example. The student writes his or her name and address on the cover. He or she writes one friend's name and address per page using the map as a reference.

Thinking it over:

Discussion questions:

1. Who lives in a ranch house?
2. Who lives in an apartment?
3. Who lives in a one story house?
4. How many students live in a brick house? Wood? Metal?
5. What ways are all houses alike?
6. What ways are they different?
7. How many students live on _____ (name) street?
8. How many students can walk to school?

One step beyond activities:

1. Make flashcards of the students' addresses. See how many addresses the students can recognize including their own.
2. Address Books: These can be made in the following ways:
    a. When you are finished with the bulletin board activity "Where We Live," compile the students' house pictures including their addresses into a class address book.
    b. You might want to arrange field trips to photograph the outside of each student's home. The students can compare likenesses and differences in house styles and designs. The students and you will gain a better understanding of each other. Mount the photographs onto pages in an album. Each student can label his or her page with the correct name and address.

Where We Live

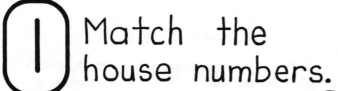

1 Match the house numbers.

2 Make an address book.

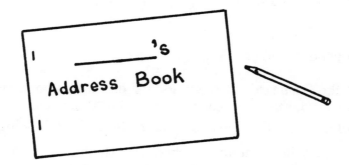

File Folder Directions

TEACHER'S DIRECTIONS FOR "MY FAMILY TREE" CENTER

Content areas: Social studies, motor

Skills: Classifying, self-image, coordination

Materials needed:

  Paper
  Pencils
  Crayons
  Tape
  Teacher-made patterns

Materials preparation:

- Cut one strip of paper approximately 30″ × 48″ per student. It is helpful to roll, paper clip, and stand the paper in a box at this area.
- Duplicate a copy of the leaf and apple patterns on heavy paper. Cut out the patterns.
- Provide a container for "My Family Tree" information sheets requested in the parent letter.

DIRECTIONS FOR FILE FOLDER ACTIVITIES:

Activity 1

The student tapes the corners of the large paper onto the floor. He or she draws a large tree with several branches on the paper.

Activity 2

The student traces the teacher's apple and leaf patterns on the bottom edge of the tree branches, making one apple and two leaves per each family member. He or she draws and labels the head of each person on the apple. Using "My Family Tree" information sheet as a reference, the student records the birthdate and birth place on the leaves.

Thinking it over:

Discussion questions:

1. Who is the oldest person in your family?
2. Who is the youngest person in your family?
3. What do you like about living in a small family?
4. What do you like about living in a large family?
5. What first or middle names have been passed down in your family?
6. Does anyone have a Grandma or Grandpa living with them?

One step beyond activities:

1. Make a class graph of the number of people in the students' families. You may wish to graph the students' position in their families (oldest child, youngest child, middle child, or only child).
2. The students can draw pictures of their families arranging the family members from youngest to oldest.
3. Older person–student interviews. Ask the students to choose one person in their family who is at least 40 years older than them. The student should interview the person (tape recorders would be acceptable) to find out: person's birthplace, birthdate, games played when the person was the student's age, types of transportation, favorite toys, weekend activities, family jobs, vacations, allowances, and so on. Arrange times for the students to share the interview information. You may wish to schedule this activity over a multi-day span with a few students participating each day.

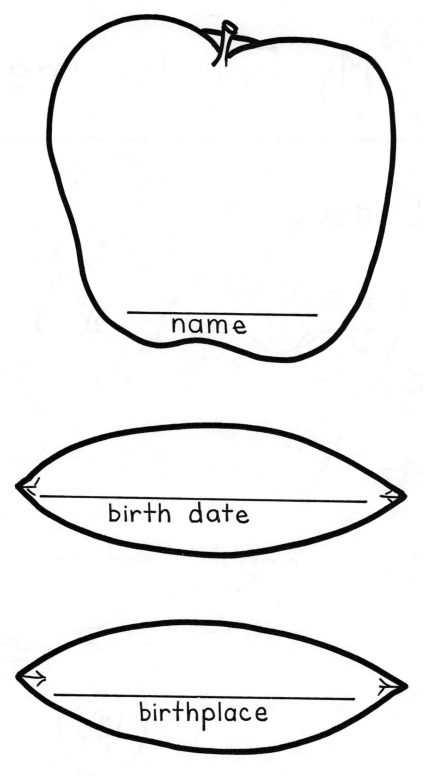

name

birth date

birthplace

Patterns

My Family Tree

1 Draw a tree.

My Family Tree

Crayons

Family Tree Information ②

2 Draw apples and leaves.

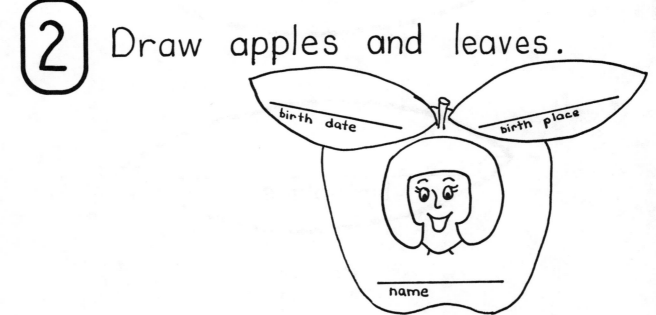

birth date

birth place

name

File Folder Directions

TEACHER'S DIRECTIONS FOR "FAMILY BIRTHDAYS" CENTER

Content areas: Math, motor

Skills: Time (months), ordinal numbers, coordination, matching

Materials needed:

>   Copies of student activity page
>   Scissors
>   Pencil
>   Crayons
>   Paste
>   One piece of 12″ × 18″ construction paper per student
>   Teacher-made birthday candle matching game and envelope

Materials preparation:

1. Make a birthday candle matching game by cutting out the candle pattern shown below and tracing around it twelve times on oaktag.

Make 12 candles   candle pattern

On each candle write the name of a month. Write the matching ordinal number on the opposite end (flame part). Cut each candle apart differently to make the game self-checking.

2. Use a copy of the student activity page to make an envelope for the game. You may prefer to write the names of the twelve months on the envelope for younger students to copy. Laminate the game and the envelope.

3. Students will need to borrow "My Family Tree" information sheets from "My Family Tree" Center for envelope birthdate references.

DIRECTIONS FOR FILE FOLDER ACTIVITIES:

Activity 1

The student plays teacher-made birthday candle game.

Activity 2

The student makes his or her own birthday candle game referring to the teacher's game.

Activity 3

He or she cuts, folds, and pastes sides of the student activity page to form an envelope. He or she writes the first six months on one side of the envelope and the remaining six months on the opposite side.
The student writes the name and birthday for each family member opposite the birth month, referring to the "My Family Tree" information sheet.

Thinking it over:

Discussion questions:

1. How do you celebrate birthdays in your family?
2. What was the best birthday you ever had? Why?
3. What things can you do to make a family member's birthday special?
4. What can you give a family member that does not cost any money?
5. How many months begin with J? What are they?
6. How many months end with y? What are they?

One step beyond activities:

1. Make a class graph of students birthdays/months. Discuss how many students have birthdays in July. What month has the most birthdays in our class? What month has the least?
2. Have each student plan a surprise party for someone in their family. Where would they hold the party? Who would they invite? What would they eat? Who would help them keep the party a secret?
3. Provide calendars for each of the students to write their family members birthdays. Grandparents, Aunts, Uncles, and Cousins could be included. Encourage the students to send hand-made cards to their relatives. (You will need to request birthday information from the parents prior to scheduling this activity.)
4. Make a "Names of Months" chart. List names of months and their origins on it.

Family Birthdays

1 Match the birthday candles.

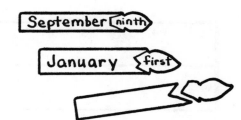

2

Make your own game.

3 Make the envelope.

_____'s Family Birthday List

January		
February		
March		
April		
May		
June		

paste

File Folder Directions

_____'s Family Birthdays List

months of the year:	family member:	birth date:
January		
		July

(lower portion rotated 180°)

months of the year:	family member:	birth date:

Student Activity Page

TEACHER'S DIRECTIONS FOR "WANTS AND NEEDS" CENTER

Content areas: Social studies, motor

Skills: Classifying, comparing, coordination

Materials needed:

      Copies of student activity page
      Pencil
      Crayons
      Paste
      One large paper bag per student
      Magazines and catalogs

Materials preparation:

Be sure the students understand that families have wants and needs. (Conduct group discussion, listing basic needs on the chalkboard, and so on.)

DIRECTIONS FOR FILE FOLDER ACTIVITIES:

Activity 1

Using a copy of the student activity page, the student colors, cuts out, sorts, and pastes pictures onto the three needs categories.

Activity 2

The student cuts out and pastes magazine pictures of things his family wants onto a paper bag.

Optional activity

The student may make lists of things or draw pictures about the emotional needs of his or her family, such as love, happiness, fun, helping each other, sharing, and so on.

Thinking it over:

Discussion questions:

1. What do you need to live?
2. What are some things that your family wants?
3. What ways do you have to get things?
4. How does your family get money to buy what they need and want?
5. How do you help?
6. Who decides what to buy for your family?

One step beyond activities:

1. "Wants and Needs" Bingo Game: The game may be played by the entire class. You will need to:
    a. Write a list of 16 items on the chalkboard (some "wants" and some "needs") such as: T.V., water, telephone, food, happiness, home, clothing, car, pop, radio, love, air, peace, bike, fun, and roller skates.

    b. Have each student fold a 9″ × 12″ piece of paper into a 16 box format, then line the folds with a pencil.

    c. Have each student copy the list of 16 items in random order onto his or her paper.

    d. Provide small squares of paper for the students to use to cover the answers on their word paper.

    e. Write the 16 words on 3″ × 5″ index cards. Provide a container for them.

    f. Play "Needs" Bingo. You or a designated student draw and read a card to the class. If the word is a "need" the student covers it with a marker. The student who has four correct words in a row wins. Vary the game by using "want" words, and so on.

2. Creative writing. Some ideas are: "If I had $50.00 I would buy my family _____." "My Dad and I went grocery shopping on Saturday for foods my family needed. We bought _____." "If I could buy my own clothes for school, I would _____."

Wants and Needs

1 Do the ditto.

2 Paste things your family wants on a bag.

File Folder Directions

My Family Needs

Food	Clothing	Home

name _____

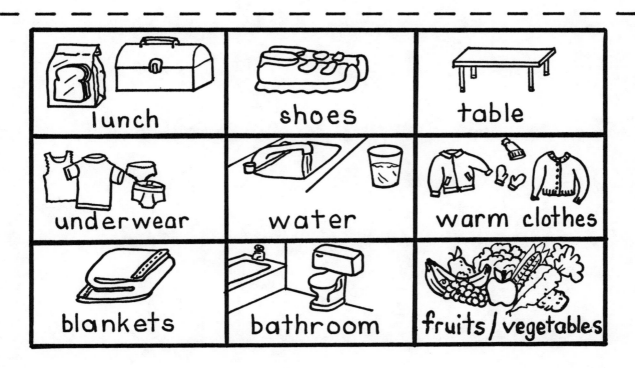

lunch	shoes	table
underwear	water	warm clothes
blankets	bathroom	fruits / vegetables

Student Activity Page

TEACHER'S DIRECTIONS FOR THE "FAMILY FUN" CENTER

Content areas: Social studies, communication, motor

Skills: Using reference materials, creative writing, art

Materials needed:

    Easel
    Paints
    Paintbrushes
    Paper
    Pencil
    References (pictionary–dictionary)

DIRECTIONS FOR FILE FOLDER ACTIVITIES:

Activity 1

The student writes a story: "My Family Has Fun," using the available references.

Activity 2

The student paints a picture about his or her story.

Thinking it over:

Discussion questions:

1. What activities does your family like to do indoors?
2. What activities does your family like to do outdoors?
3. What does your family like to do on weekends?
4. Where does your family like to go on vacation?
5. Who decides where you will go on vacation?

One step beyond activities:

1. "Family Fun" bulletin board. Ask each student to bring a photograph or draw a picture depicting his or her family in a fun activity. Give the students an opportunity to discuss the pictures.
2. Play "Family Fun" Charades. Divide the class into pairs. Provide a stack of 3″ × 5″ index cards with activity words written on them, such as: watching T.V., cooking, soccer, gardening, roller skating, swimming, going to the zoo, going to the library, going to the museum, shopping, playing computer games, building things, and so on. Each pair of students draws a card and acts out the activity listed. Other students guess the activity being portrayed.

Family Fun

1 Write "My family has fun..."

My family has fun when ____

2 Paint a picture about your story.

File Folder Directions

TEACHER'S DIRECTIONS FOR "INSIDE MY HOUSE" CENTER

(Open-ended activity)

Content areas: Communication, teacher's choice

Skills: Listening, vocabulary development, teacher's choice

Materials needed:

> Teacher-made matching game
> Copies of student activity page
> Pencil
> Paper
> Crayons
> References: pictionary–dictionary
> Tape recorder
> Cassette tape
> A book about houses such as: Schlein, Miriam, *My House,* Albert Whitman and Co., Chicago, 1971. Oppenheim, Joanne, *Have You Seen Houses?,* Young Scott Books, Addison-Wesley Co., Reading, Mass., 1973. Le Sieg, Theo., *In a People House,* Random House, Inc. New York, 1972.

Materials preparation:

1. Tape record the book you have chosen for this center.
2. Make a matching game using objects or pictures–objects of things you can find in a house. (*In A People House* is an excellent reference.) Some ideas are:
   A. Rhyming words: pail-nail, clock-sock, pan-can, ring-string, book-hook, T.V.-key, lamp-stamp, bed-thread.
   B. Words that go together: cup-saucer, pencil-paper, fork-spoon, hammer-nail, shoe-sock, needle-thread, salt-pepper, pan-lid. Laminate pictures and provide container for the game.
3. Determine skill you wish to reinforce for the student activity page, such as: student can draw pictures in the windows of House A and rhyming pictures in the windows of House B, draw pictures in the windows of House A and write rhyming words in the windows of House B, or write rhyming words in the windows of Houses A and B. Student can draw lines between matching windows.

DIRECTIONS FOR FILE FOLDER ACTIVITIES:

Activity 1

The student listens to the story.

Activity 2

The student plays the matching game.

Activity 3

The student completes the student activity page as per your directions using references.

Thinking it over:

Discussion questions:

1. What objects in the classroom rhyme?
2. What classroom objects start with "c"?
3. What classroom objects end with "k"?
4. What classroom objects do you also have in your home?
5. What classroom objects do you not have in your home?

One step beyond activities:

1. Make *My Home* books. You determine the number of pages and pre-staple if necessary. Each student draws the front of his or her home on the front cover and writes his or her name and address. On the back cover the student draws the back view of his or her home. Then the student labels the inside pages: living room, kitchen, bedroom, and so on. The student may draw pictures of objects he or she has in the rooms of his or her home. The students may label the objects using pictionaries or dictionaries for references.
2. The students can write the letters of the alphabet vertically on paper. He or she may use a dictionary or pictionary to list household objects that begin with each letter.

Inside My House

1 Listen to the book.

2 Play the game.

2 Matching Game

3 Do the ditto.

File Folder Directions

House A

House B

name_____

Student Activity Page

TEACHER'S DIRECTIONS FOR "FAMILY JOBS" CENTER

Content areas: Social studies, motor

Skills: Self-image, creating, sort-matching

Materials needed:

Teacher-made placemat
Teacher-made example paper
Pencil
Paper
Crayons
Scissors
Enough 12″ × 18″ heavy paper for each student and his or her family members
Five of each of the following table setting items: napkins, plates, cups, knives, spoons, and forks.

Materials preparation:

1. Make an example 12″ × 18″ paper (folded into quarters) as pictured on the file folder directions.
   On one side write "Ways I help my family," on the opposite side write "Ways my family helps me."
2. To make a placemat, glue, tape, or staple one of each of the table setting items (paper or plastic) on a 12″ × 18″ paper. The example will show the proper way to set the table service. Some ideas for placemats are paper weaving, border designs, fringing, and so on.

DIRECTIONS FOR FILE FOLDER ACTIVITIES:

Activity 1

The student draws pictures and may write sentences to complete the "Ways I help . . ." paper, referring to your example.

Activity 2

The student makes a placemat for each family member. He or she sets the table with the table service, referring to your placemat.

Thinking it over:

Discussion questions:

1. What jobs do you do inside your home?
2. What jobs do you do outside your home?
3. What jobs do you share with other people in your family?
4. Why do you share the above jobs?
5. What job do you like to do best?
6. What job do you like to do least?
7. Who decides what jobs your family members do?

One step beyond activities:

1. "What's My Job?" game: Divide the class into pairs. Provide a stack of 3″ × 5″ index cards with different kinds of jobs written on them, such as: making beds, washing dishes, taking out the trash, doing laundry, vacuuming carpets, dusting, baking cookies, making pizza, mowing lawn, raking leaves, washing cars, walking dog, and so on. Each pair of students draws a card and acts out the job described. Other students guess the job being portrayed.
2. Students can write letters to their parents suggesting new jobs they would like to try doing at home. Encourage them to share ideas on rotating, sharing, and scheduling new and old jobs.

Family Jobs

1 Make the paper.

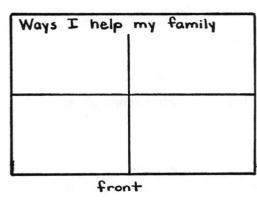

Ways I help my family

front

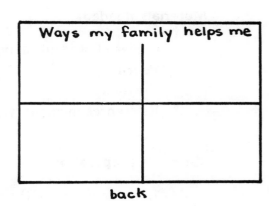

Ways my family helps me

back

2 Make placemats for your family. Set the table.

File Folder Directions

TEACHER'S DIRECTIONS FOR "MY FAVORITE RELATIVE" CENTER

Content areas: Communication, motor

Skills: Letter writing, handwriting

Materials needed:

     Copies of student activity page
     Pencil
     Crayons
     References: pictionary–dictionary, teacher-made chart

Materials preparation:

     1. Using a copy of the student activity page, make an example letter for the younger student, such as:

```
                                    _____
                                          date

Dear _____,
   I am writing a letter to my favorite relative. Can you guess
who?

                      Love,

                  _____
```

     2. Make a reference chart for older students to use with correct placement of date, salutation, body, closing, and signature.
     3. Address an envelope showing correct placement of return address, address, and stamp.
     4. Provide a container for the student's favorite relative addresses and stamped envelopes which were requested in the parent letter.

DIRECTIONS FOR FILE FOLDER ACTIVITIES:

Activity 1

Using a copy of the student activity page, the student writes a letter to a favorite relative using references. He or she may color the pictures on the student activity page.

Activity 2

The student addresses his or her envelope. The student may mail his or her letter at school, home, or post office.

Thinking it over:

Discussion questions:

1. How did you choose the relative you wrote to?
2. How often do you see that relative?
3. Do you know where (state, country) your relative lives?
4. How long will it take your letter to reach your relative?
5. Why do you need a zip code?

One step beyond activities:

1. Display a map on the bulletin board. Provide map pins and small pieces of paper. Each student writes his or her name on the paper and pins it to the destination area of his or her letter. Encourage students to share any communications they receive from their relatives. You may wish to have the students place a different colored map pin on the map when they receive a response.
2. Schedule a class field trip to your local post office. You may want to save all of the class letters until the trip so the students can mail them. Arrange to have a conducted tour of the post office. Give the students an opportunity to ask questions about the various postal functions. Follow-up trip activities could include writing thank you notes and experience stories.
3. Encourage students to write to other relatives in their families.

 # My Favorite Relative

1 Write a letter to a favorite relative.

2 Address the envelope.

your name

address

city   state
              zip code

name

address

city   state
              zip code

File Folder Directions

COUSIN- UNCLE- GRANDMOTHER- MAMA- GRANDPA- DADDY- STEP FATHER- GRANNY-

GRANDFATHER-MOM- SISTER- DAD-BROTHER- NEPHEW- NIECE- STEP MOTHER- AUNT-

Student Activity Page

TEACHER'S DIRECTIONS FOR "FAMILY" ENRICHMENT ACTIVITIES

"Family" Group Activity

Family Buffet Lunch

"Family" Home Activity

Duplicate the pages on colored paper. Send the pages home ten days prior to the Family Buffet Lunch. Encourage the students to contribute recipes for the class recipe book.

"Family" Awards

Duplicate the pages on colored paper. Give each child who returns the Family Home Activity a Home Activity Award. The other Family Awards may be used for the recognition of good work, and so on.

"Family" Summary Activity

You may duplicate the Family Summary page for older students to complete independently. You may use the page for discussion questions with younger students.

"FAMILY" GROUP ACTIVITIES

You may want to revise the letter to parents (refer to p. 84) regarding the buffet lunch. You may prefer to have a family buffet dinner in the evening or a lunch for students only.

Prior to sending the letter to parents, you will need to discuss balanced meals, favorite family foods, and the recipe book with your students. List the food categories for a buffet lunch, such as: salad, vegetable, meat, and dessert on chart paper. Determine the number of dishes you will need for each category. Encourage the students to volunteer to bring food dishes for the appropriate categories. Write the requested food dish on the letter to parents. Make arrangements to provide milk and other beverages.

On the day of the buffet lunch, the students can make placemats for the family members who are planning to attend. Each student also can make his or her recipe book cover.

You may want to have parents help compile the recipe books following the buffet lunch. Stack the recipe book pages, duplicated in advance on tables. Arrange the students in an assembly line to pick up the pages and put on the covers. Parents could help staple or tie the books together.

FAVORITE FOODS

Date _____

Dear Parent,
    We are planning to have a buffet lunch at school on _____
_____ at _____. We would like to
have you and your family come. Please bring your child's favorite _____
_____ dish (_____ servings), utensils, and table service for your
family (cups, plates, knives, forks, spoons, napkins). Please label your dishes
with your name. Milk, _____ will be furnished.
    We will look forward to seeing you at the buffet lunch. It will be a good
family sharing experience. In order to plan table and seating space, please return
the bottom part of this note by _____.

Sincerely,

Your child's teacher

_____ Number of family members planning to attend the buffet lunch
             on _____.
_____ I cannot attend, but I would be willing to send a
             _____ dish and table service for my child.

_____   _____
      Child's name   *Your Signature*

Our

Favorite

Foods

"FAMILY" HOME ACTIVITY ENRICHMENT PAGE

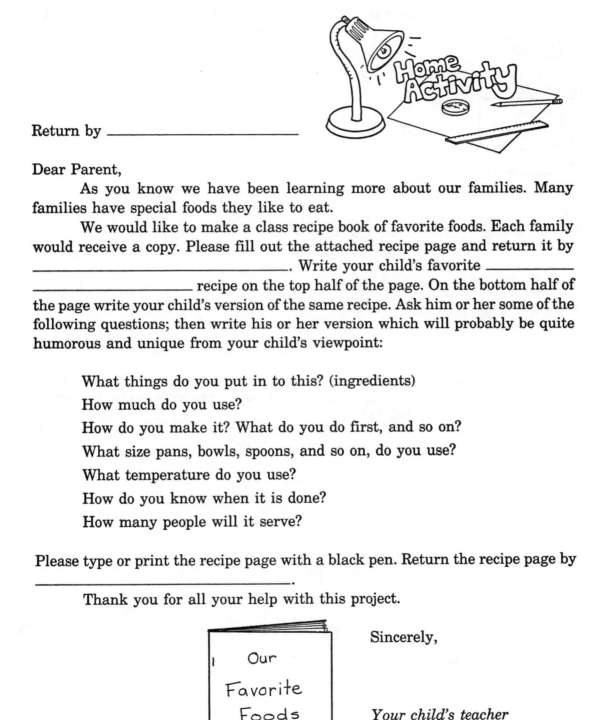

Return by _____

Dear Parent,

As you know we have been learning more about our families. Many families have special foods they like to eat.

We would like to make a class recipe book of favorite foods. Each family would receive a copy. Please fill out the attached recipe page and return it by _____. Write your child's favorite _____ _____ recipe on the top half of the page. On the bottom half of the page write your child's version of the same recipe. Ask him or her some of the following questions; then write his or her version which will probably be quite humorous and unique from your child's viewpoint:

What things do you put in to this? (ingredients)

How much do you use?

How do you make it? What do you do first, and so on?

What size pans, bowls, spoons, and so on, do you use?

What temperature do you use?

How do you know when it is done?

How many people will it serve?

Please type or print the recipe page with a black pen. Return the recipe page by _____.

Thank you for all your help with this project.

Sincerely,

Our Favorite Foods

Your child's teacher

_____ **RECIPE**

From the Kitchen of _____**'s Family**

child's full name

_____ would prepare the recipe this way:

child's full name

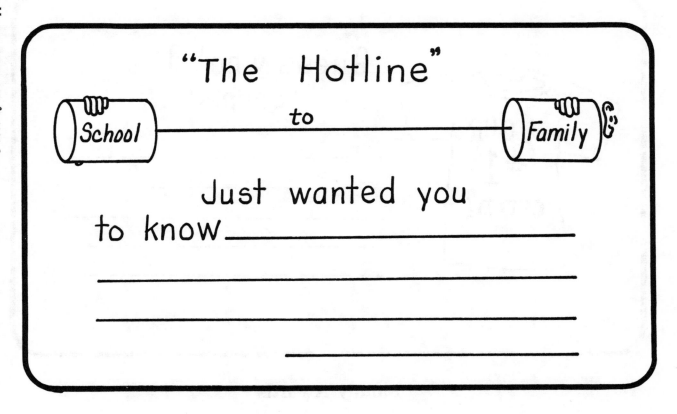

child _____

parent _____

Thank you for completing the Family Home Activity.

Our Favorite Foods

_____
teacher

Home Activity Award

"The Hotline"

School — to — Family

Just wanted you to know_____

_____

_____

_____

Family Award

Brag it up!

Tell the whole family...

GRANDPA, AUNT, SISTER, GRANDMA, DAD, UNCLE, BROTHER, MOM, COUSIN

Guess what I've learned..

YOUR #1 CHILD!

Family Awards

"FAMILY" SUMMARY PAGE

Name _____

Date _____

1. What is your address? _____
                               number   *street*

   _____
           city   *state*   *zip code*

2. List the names of the people in your family: _____

   _____

   _____

3. What is your birthdate? _____ _____ _____
                           month   *day*   *year*

4. List the three things that your family needs to live:

   a. _____ b. _____ c. _____

5. List three things that your family wants:

   a. _____ b. _____ c. _____

6. What does your family like to do for fun? _____

   _____

   _____

   _____

7. List four objects in your house that you use everyday:

   a. _____ b. _____

   c. _____ d. _____

8. What is one way you help your family? _____

   _____

9. What is one way your family helps you? _____

   _____

10. Who is your favorite relative? _____

School

SCHOOL

4 5

3 6

2 7

1 8

Center Marker

"SCHOOL" CENTER MARKER

A learning center marker is provided for students using the Social Studies unit at learning centers. (Refer to page 230.)

Distribute copies of the "School" markers to the students. The students can color and cut out their markers and place them near the "School" Learning Centers.

SCHOOL DAYS

Date _____

Dear Parent,

School activities will be the focus of our new social studies unit. Your child will become more aware of his or her school schedules, workers, rules, and surroundings.

A map of our classroom will be on the bulletin board. Your child will make a similar map showing classroom symbol arrangements and cardinal directions. He or she will follow tape recorded directions to trace routes within the classroom. Map skills emphasized will be using a compass, labeling a compass rose, using symbols, and routing. You may want to extend these activities at home by letting your child use a compass and planning routes within your home.

Playground, school, and classroom rules will be reviewed at the School Rules learning center. You may want to discuss other rules with your child.

Math skills featured in these school activities are: learning the days of the week in order, and telling time.

We will be interviewing several people who work at our school during the next two weeks. Encourage your child to share this information with you.

Sincerely,

Your child's teacher

Date _____

From Home
To School

Dear _____,

_____
_____
_____
_____
_____
_____
_____
_____
_____
_____
_____
_____

_____
Parent Signature

Dear Parent,

    I would appreciate any feedback you or your child may have regarding the "School" Social Studies activities: My Classroom, My School Book, School Days, Substitute Teacher, School Rules, My Backpack, My Week, and Hide and Seek.

    Please use this page for comments and return it to me by _____.

        Sincerely,

        Your child's teacher

"SCHOOL" LEARNING CENTERS LIST

This Social studies unit includes a variety of school-oriented activities.

"My Classroom" Center

(A bulletin board is used with this activity.)

Content areas: Social studies, communication

Skills: Mapping, routing, listening, comparing

Activities:

1. Arrange the classroom symbols on the map.
2. Follow tape recorded directions to complete the student activity page.

"My School Book" Center

Content areas: Communication, motor, social studies

Skills: Creative writing, creating, self-image

Activities:

1. Make a book.
2. Write and illustrate the pages.

"School Days" Center

Content areas: Math, motor

Skills: Measurement (time), coordination, handwriting

Activities:

1. Make a poster.
2. Draw hands on each clock on the poster.

"Substitute Teacher" Center

Content areas: Communication, motor

Skills: Listening, creating, creative writing

Activities:

1. Listen to the cassette tape of the book.
2. Write a creative story, "If I were a substitute teacher . . ."

"School Rules" Center

Content areas: Social studies, motor

Skills: Classifying, handwriting, creating

Activities:

1. Draw faces on the student activity page.
2. Write one rule and illustrate it.

"My Backpack" Center

(Open-ended activity)

Content areas: Motor, teacher's choice

Skills: Handwriting, coordination, teacher's choice, matching

Activities:

1. Color and cut out the backpack.
2. Insert strips into backpack, write words on strips.

"My Week" Center

Content areas: Social studies, math, motor

Skills: Using reference materials, measurement (time), handwriting, coordination

Activities:

1. Write days of the week on the chalkboard.
2. Make a chain using the strips on the student activity page.

"Hide and Seek" Center

Content areas: Social studies, communication, motor

Skills: Using reference materials, spelling, vocabulary development, handwriting

Activities:

1. Collect hidden objects in the room.
2. Write and draw pictures of objects.

TEACHER'S DIRECTIONS FOR "MY CLASSROOM" CENTER

Content areas: Social studies, communication

Skills: Mapping, routing, listening, comparing

Materials needed:

> Bulletin board
> Copies of student activity page
> Tape recorder
> Cassette tape
> Teacher-made classroom symbols cards and envelope
> Thumbtacks and container
> Compass
> Pencil
> Crayons

Materials preparation:

1. Make "My Classroom" bulletin board map as pictured on the file folder directions page.
2. Make a set of classroom picture symbols on 3″ × 5″ index cards for the bulletin board. Include the six symbols on the student activity page, as well as others appropriate for your classroom, such as windows, doors, and student desks. You may also want to add windows and doors on the student activity page prior to duplicating student copies.
3. Establish background enabling the student to use a compass, label cardinal directions on a compass rose, and follow routes within your classroom.
4. Prepare a cassette tape of directions for the student activity page, such as:

> Use the compass to find North.
> Label the compass rose, write N for North, S for South, E for East, and W for West on the student activity page.
> Look at the symbols at the bottom of the page.
> Draw the symbols at the correct places on your classroom map. (*Optional:* older students can label the symbols.)
> Give appropriate routing directions for your classroom.

Some ideas are:

> Make a blue line to show the shortest route from the flag to the teacher's desk.
> Make a red line to show the longest route from the waste basket to the reading table.

DIRECTIONS FOR FILE FOLDER ACTIVITIES:

Activity 1

The student will tack the classroom symbols at the corresponding locations on the classroom bulletin board map.

Activity 2

The student will follow your tape recorded directions to complete the student activity page.

Thinking it over:

Discussion questions:

1. How many windows are there in our classroom?
2. How many doors are there in our classroom?
3. What walls have windows? (North, South, East, West)
4. What walls have doors?
5. What color is the floor?
6. What kind of floor covering is there?
7. How many desks are there in our classroom?
8. How many bookcases are there in our classroom?
9. Why is the furniture arranged this way?
10. What ways would you arrange the furniture? Why?

One step beyond activities:

1. Arrange to visit another classroom in your school when there are no students in it. Encourage your students to look for specific details such as furniture arrangement, number of doors, number of windows, floor coverings, and so on. Follow-up activities could include room comparison discussion and making charts listing the classroom likenesses and differences.
2. The student can fold a piece of 12″ by 18″ paper into a four box format, then label the boxes: North, South, East, and West. He or she draws pictures or writes the names of objects found on each wall of your classroom in the appropriate box.
3. Discuss or prepare a worksheet of the following ideas:
   a. Name one triangular-shaped object in our room.
   b. Name the color of the West wall.
   c. Name six rectangular objects.
   d. Name three things that can open and close.
   e. Name an object that is in the middle of our room.
   f. Name three objects that are above your head.
   g. Name four objects that are round.

My Classroom

My   Classroom

classroom symbols

1 Arrange the furniture.

2 Listen to the tape.
Do the ditto.

File Folder Directions

compass rose

Put these symbols on your map as they are in your classroom.

○ wastebasket   🕐 clock

▤ bookcase   📖 reading table

🍎 teacher's desk   🏴 flag

name

Student Activity Page

TEACHER'S DIRECTIONS FOR "MY SCHOOL BOOK" CENTER

Content areas: Communication, motor, Social studies

Skills: Creative writing, creating, self-image

Materials needed:

    Student activity pattern
Paper: wallpaper, notebook, handwriting, construction
Pencil
Crayons
Stapler–staples
Scissors
Teacher-made book

Materials preparation:

1. Establish background information regarding the "shape" of the school book outline (refer to the student activity page), if necessary.
2. Make a school book using copies of the student activity page. The book is designed with one or two sentences and illustrations per page. Some ideas are:

        My name is _____.
        I go to _____ school.
        My school's address is _____.
        My school was built in _____.
        I travel to school by _____.
        My school has _____ rooms.
        My favorite room is _____.
        I am in _____ grade in Room _____.
        My teacher is _____.
        At recess, I like to _____.

You need to determine:

1. Number of pages in book (older student can do several).
2. Type of paper for cover and content pages.
3. Way to assemble book: Older student may cut and trace student activity page for his or her cover and content pages, staple the pages together, write and illustrate pages referring to your example book. You may prefer to prepare and staple a book for the younger student to use. Make copies of the student activity page with one open-ended sentence written on each page. He or she may complete the sentences and illustrate the pages. You or an aide may help students with words at a pre-arranged time.

DIRECTIONS FOR FILE FOLDER ACTIVITIES:

Activity 1

The student assembles his or her book as per your directions.

Activity 2

The student writes and illustrates the pages.

Thinking it over:

Discussion questions:

1. How old is our school?
2. How many rooms did our school have when it was built?
3. How many rooms does our school have now?
4. Who were some of the first teachers at our school?
5. What things do you like about our school?
6. What things would you like to change at our school?

One step beyond activities:

1. Make a class book about school. The student can write and illustrate, "I like _____" on one side of large paper and "I don't like _____" on the opposite side of the paper. Compile the papers into a class book.
2. Creative writing ideas:

   a. "If I ran the school, I would _____."
   b. "One day a kid rang the fire alarm _____"
   c. "If school lasted all year, I would _____."
   d. "One day I was late for school _____"
   e. "If recess lasted one hour, I would _____."

My School Book

1 Make a book about school.

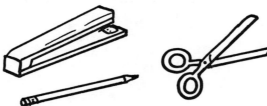

SCHOOL

pattern

2

Do each page.

File Folder Directions

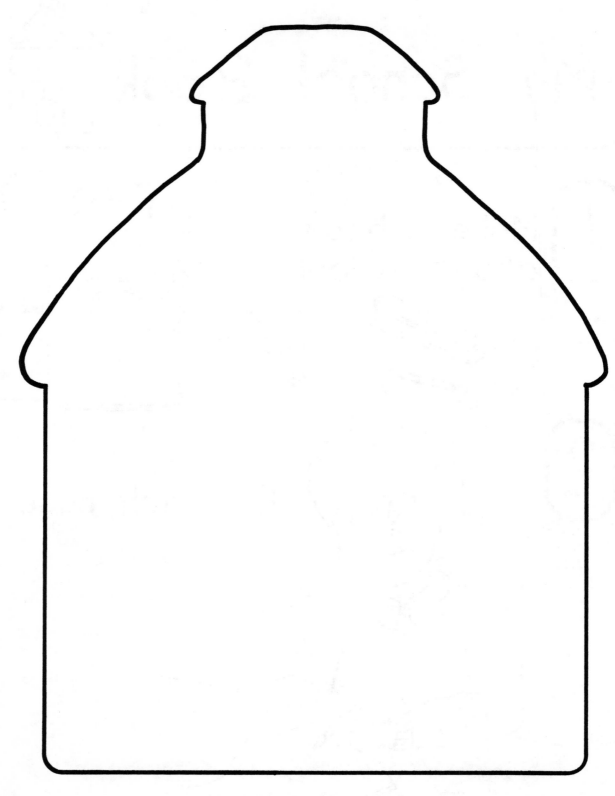

Student Activity Page

TEACHER'S DIRECTIONS FOR "SCHOOL DAYS" CENTER

Content areas: Math, motor

Skills: Measurement (time), coordination, handwriting

Materials needed:

> Copies of student activity page
> Pencil
> Scissors
> Paste
> Red permanent marking pen
> Black permanent marking pen
> Meterstick or yardstick
> One 22" × 28" light colored posterboard per student
> Teacher-made example poster

Materials preparation:

Make a "School Days" poster as pictured on the file folder directions. Using one or more copies of the student activity page, cut out and paste clocks in each column on the poster (one per daily activity). Under each clock write the daily activity and time it occurs such as, "Lunch, 12:00 p.m." You may wish to draw the clock hands for the younger student, using a red marking pen for the hour hands and a black marking pen for the minute hands. Laminate the poster.

DIRECTIONS FOR FILE FOLDER ACTIVITIES:

Activity 1

The student makes a "School Days" poster by copying all of the written information from your example poster.

Activity 2

The student cuts out the clocks on the student activity page. He or she pastes the clocks on the poster referring to your poster. He or she draws the hands on the clocks using a red pen for the four hands and a black pen for the minute hands to show the corresponding times.

Thinking it over:

Discussion questions:

1. What activities do we have at the same time every school day?
2. What is one subject that we study in the morning?
3. What is one subject that we study in the afternoon?
4. Why are the times for some activities varied?
5. Who schedules the times for Recess, Lunch, Dismissal?
6. Why is it important to have more than one Lunch hour?
7. Why is it important to have different Recess times for the classes in our school?
8. Who schedules your family's times to get up, eat meals, study, watch T.V., and go to bed? Why?
9. Do you ever help choose the time to get up and go to bed?

One step beyond activities:

1. The students can make time books, writing and illustrating the activities they do at specific times at their homes. Some ideas are: get up, eat breakfast, go to school, return from school, play outside, eat supper, do homework, watch T.V., go to bed.
2. Make a class graph to compare the times that students get up or go to bed.
3. Read the book by Brandenberg, Franz, *No School Today!*, Scholastic, Inc., New York, 1975. Follow-up activities may include: discussion, sequencing, writing stories about events the students have experienced when they were too early or too late for school.

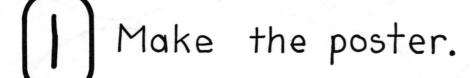

School Days

1 Make the poster.

2 Cut and paste the clocks. Draw on the hands.

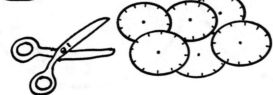 

File Folder Directions

Student Activity Page

TEACHER'S DIRECTIONS FOR "SUBSTITUTE TEACHER" CENTER

Content areas: Communication, motor

Skills: Listening, creating, creative writing

Materials needed:

Pencil
Copies of the student activity page
Crayons
Cassette tape
Tape recorder
A book about substitute teachers such as: Allard, Harry, and Marshall, James, *Miss Nelson Is Missing!* Houghton Mifflin Co., Boston, 1977, or, Allard, Harry, and Marshall, James, *Miss Nelson Is Back*, Houghton Mifflin Co., Boston, 1982.

Materials preparation:

Tape-record the book you have chosen.

DIRECTIONS FOR FILE FOLDER ACTIVITIES:

Activity 1

The student listens to the cassette tape of the book.

Activity 2

The student writes a creative story, "If I were a substitute teacher . . . ," on the student activity page referring to the vocabulary. He or she illustrates the story on the back of the student activity page.

Thinking it over:

Discussion questions:

1. What is the first thing you think about when you see a substitute teacher in our classroom?
2. What do you like about having a substitute teacher?
3. What don't you like about having a substitute teacher?
4. What happens if you don't work for a substitute teacher?
5. Where do you think substitute teachers come from to teach?
6. Who telephones substitute teachers?

One step beyond activities:

1. Make a substitute teacher chart. Ask the students to think of ways they could help a substitute teacher; write them on large chart paper, and post the chart in your room.
2. Make a class book. Compile student's stories or pictures about "One day, our teacher was sick and no one came to substitute teach. This is what I did _____."

Substitute Teacher

1 Listen to the book.

2 Do the ditto.

If I were
a substitute teacher

File Folder Directions

decide
reward
would easy
try listen
whisper
happy tell
fair
quiet
wonderful
warn
principal
list
talk
school
last
excuse
hard
helpful
first
students
noise
begin
recess
finish
give
extra
ask
because

If I were
a substitute teacher

_____

_____

_____

_____

_____

_____

_____

_____

_____

_____

_____

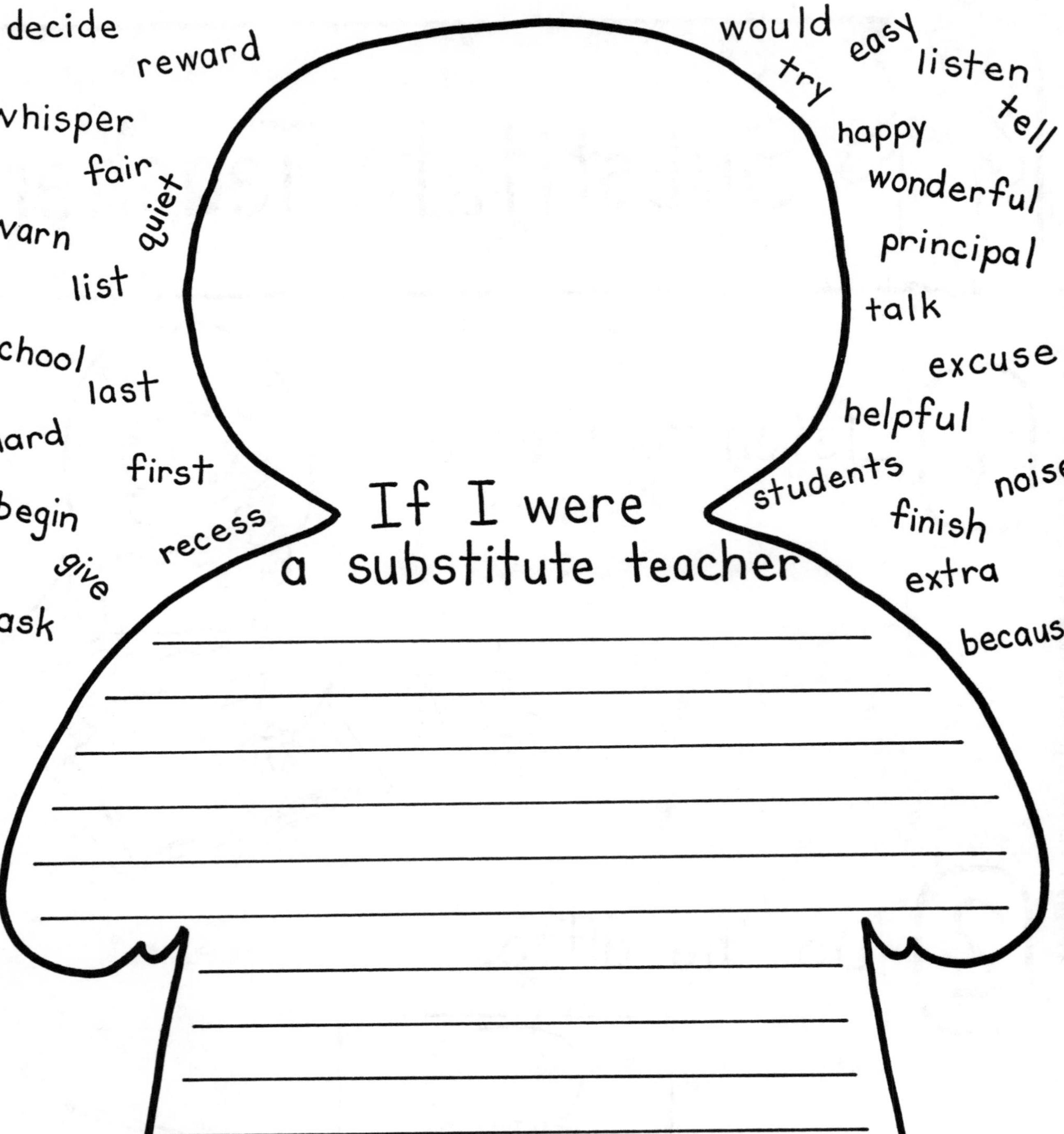

_____
name

Student Activity Page

TEACHER'S DIRECTIONS FOR "SCHOOL RULES" CENTER

Content areas: Social studies, motor

Skills: Classifying, charting, handwriting, creating

Materials needed:

> Copies of student activity page
> Pencil
> Crayons
> Paper

Materials preparation:

Discuss playground, school, and classroom rules with your students. You may want to make a chart of the rules which are on the student activity page. As an aid to beginning readers you may prepare a cassette tape of the rules on the student activity page.

DIRECTIONS FOR FILE FOLDER ACTIVITIES:

Activity 1

The student completes the student activity page by drawing a happy face or a sad face in the appropriate categories for each rule.

Activity 2

The student writes one rule and illustrates it. Older students may do more than one rule.

Thinking it over:

Discussion questions:

1. What are rules?
2. Why do people need to make rules?
3. What are some of the rules for the playground?
4. What are some of the rules for inside our school?
5. How are rules at home different from rules at school?
6. How are the rules alike?
7. Who made the rules at home?
8. What are some important rules to follow at home?
9. What are some rules you might give grownups to follow?

One step beyond activities:

1. Review the meaning of the Constitution of the United States with the class. The students can understand that our government follows a set of rules called the Constitution, whereas the students follow a set of school rules. Let the students make a classroom "constitution" giving reasons for rules. Then let each student sign it.
2. Play "Rules Charades." Divide the class into pairs. The students take turns pantomining school rules for the class to guess.

School Rules

1 Do the ditto.

2 Write a rule.
Make a picture about it.

File Folder Directions

School Rules

☺ = good rule   ☹ = bad rule

	PLAY-GROUND	SCHOOL	ROOM
1. I sit on the swing.			
2. I run in the hall.			
3. I do neat work.			
4. I keep my desk clean.			
5. I stand on the slide.			
6. I throw paper.			
7. I finish work on time.			
8. I push kids in lines.			
9. I work quietly.			
10. I help new students.			

name

Student Activity Page

TEACHER'S DIRECTIONS FOR "MY BACKPACK" CENTER

(Open-ended activity)

Content areas: Motor, teacher's choice

Skills: Handwriting, coordination, teacher's choice, matching

Materials needed:

Copies of student activity page (duplicate on heavy paper)
Pencil
Scissors
Crayons
One 2″ × 18″ strip of yellow construction paper per student
One 2″ × 18″ strip of orange construction paper per student
Teacher-made strip examples

Materials preparation:

- Determine a skill to reinforce or review, such as compound words, contractions, color words-colors, upper and lower case letters.
- Make two strip examples for the student to copy. On a 2″ × 18″ yellow strip write the words that you want to appear above the left pocket of the backpack on the student activity page, such as, "you will, do not," and so on. On a 2″ × 18″ orange strip write the words you want to appear above the right pocket of the backpack in mixed order, such as "don't, you'll," and so on.

DIRECTIONS FOR FILE FOLDER ACTIVITIES:

Activity 1

The student colors and cuts out the backpack, including the slots, on the student activity page.

Activity 2

The student inserts the yellow and orange strips into the slots on the backpack. He or she writes the words as per your examples. He or she matches the corresponding words by pulling the strips through the slots.

Thinking it over:

Discussion questions:

1. Why is it helpful to have a backpack?
2. What kinds of things do you carry in a backpack?
3. When do you fill up your backpack for school?
4. Does anyone help remind you to put things in your backpack?
5. What other things can you use to bring stuff to school?
6. Is it easier to carry things in a backpack? Why?

One step beyond activities:

1. The students can list or draw objects that can come to school in a backpack on one side of a paper. List objects that can come home from school in a backpack on the opposite side of the paper.
2. Play "What's in My Backpack?" game. Divide the class into small groups. Provide several common school objects such as pencil, eraser, lunch box, scissors, ruler, tablet, paste, crayons, folder, into individual paper bags. Place the bags into backpack (one per group). Each student takes a turn selecting one bag out of the backpack. He or she peeks at the object in his or her bag, then gives a descriptive clue to the other group members. The other students try to guess the object. The student who guesses the correct object gets the next turn to select a bag from the backpack. The group continues in this way until the backpack is empty.
3. Use audiovisual aids and books to show ways people carry things in different countries.

My Backpack

1 Make the backpack.

2 Put in the strips.
Write the words.

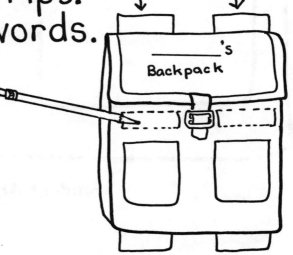

_____'s
Backpack

File Folder Directions

Student Activity Page

TEACHER'S DIRECTIONS FOR "MY WEEK" CENTER

Content areas: Social studies, math, motor

Skills: Using reference materials, measurement (time), handwriting, coordination

Materials needed:

> Copies of student activity page
> Chalkboard
> Chalk
> Pencil
> Crayons
> Scissors
> Paste
> References: calendar, pictionary–dictionary

Materials preparation:

Provide references which will enable the students to find the days of the week in order. You may write the days of the week in order on a copy of the student activity page as a reference.

DIRECTIONS FOR FILE FOLDER ACTIVITIES:

Activity 1

The student writes the days of the week in order on the chalkboard two times.

Activity 2

The student writes the days of the week in order on the student activity page. The student colors and cuts out the strips. Then he or she arranges and pastes the strips in order to form a chain.

Thinking it over:

Discussion questions:

1. What special activities do you participate in during the afternoon or evening?
2. What days are the activities held?
3. What do you like to do on Saturday and Sunday?
4. What are your favorite activities during the summer?
5. Do you have summer activities scheduled for certain days?
6. What would you do if you had an extra day off from school each week?

One step beyond activities:

1. Make a journal. The students can write about the activities they do each day for one week. The younger student may write the day of the week and draw a picture of his or her activity. Encourage the students to share one or more pages of the journal with the class.
2. Make a weekly T.V. guide. The student, referring to a calendar and newspaper, can list his or her favorite T.V. program, time, and channel for each day of the week. The younger student may write the days of the week and draw pictures of his or her favorite programs.
3. The student can list the days of the week in a column on the left side of a piece of lined paper. Encourage the student to refer to a classroom calendar to write all of the dates in the month for each day. For example: "Sunday" 1, 8, 15, 22, 29.

My Week

1 Write the days of the week on the board.

Sund

2 Make the chain.

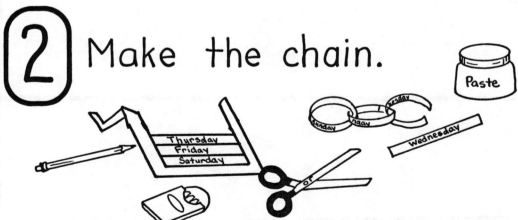

File Folder Directions

Sunday

Student Activity Page

TEACHER'S DIRECTIONS FOR "HIDE AND SEEK" CENTER

Content areas: Social studies, communication, motor

Skills: Using reference materials, spelling, vocabulary development, handwriting

Materials needed:

Pencil
Crayons
Masking tape
Red permanent marking pen
One piece of 12″ × 18″ paper per student
References: pictionary–dictionary
Timer
Collection of eight classroom objects such as pen, pencil, crayons, paper, paste, eraser, chalk, scissors
Container for objects
Teacher-made example paper

Materials preparation:

1. Make an example paper as pictured on the file folder directions page.
2. Prepare a collection of eight objects:
   a. Put pieces of masking tape which you have colored with the red permanent marking pen on the objects.
   b. Place one object at each of the eight centers or other appropriate locations in the room.
   c. Provide a container such as a shoe box, tray, or basket.
   d. Instruct the student to set the timer for three minutes when he or she arrives at the center. He or she will hunt for the hidden objects, put them in the container, and return to the center within three minutes.

DIRECTIONS FOR FILE FOLDER ACTIVITIES

Activity 1

The student collects the objects hidden in the room as per your directions.

Activity 2

The student prepares a paper as per your example. Using references, the student writes the name of each object and illustrates it. Then the student hides the eight objects in the room.

Optional activity

The older student may look for eight additional objects and record them on the opposite side of the paper.

Thinking it over:

Discussion questions:

1. What things in our classroom are the same as things in your home?
2. What things are different?
3. What things do you use everyday at school?
4. Could we call these things "tools"?
5. What tools do your parents use at home?
6. What tools do your parents use at their jobs?

One step beyond activities:

1. Prepare a tape cassette of classroom sounds such as a pencil sharpener, crayons shaken in a box, chalkboard being erased, record player, tape recorder, typewriter, clock, door being closed, chalk on a chalkboard, bell, and so on. The students take turns identifying each classroom sound. You may want to number the order of the sounds on the tape cassette. The students could write numbers in a column on paper prior to listening to the tape cassette. When the tape cassette was played, the student would record each guess with the matching number.
2. Make mobiles or collages featuring catalog or magazine pictures of common classroom objects. You may want to divide the students into small groups to cut out and paste the pictures.

Hide and Seek

1  Find the objects in the room.

2 Write words. Make pictures.

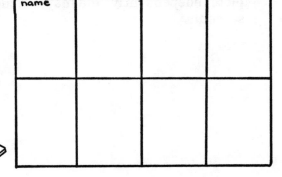

name

Hide the objects again.

File Folder Directions

TEACHER'S DIRECTIONS FOR "SCHOOL" ENRICHMENT ACTIVITIES

"School" Group Activity

School Workers Interviews

"School" Home Activity

Duplicate the pages on colored paper. Send the page home when you begin the School Social studies unit. Encourage the students to interview their parents and/or grandparents about their school activities.

"School" Awards

Duplicate the pages on colored paper. Give each child who returns the "School" Home Activity a Home Activity Award. The other Family Awards may be used for the recognition of good work, and so on.

"School" Summary Activity

You may duplicate the School Summary page for older students to complete independently. You may use the page for discussion questions with younger students.

"SCHOOL" GROUP ACTIVITIES

The purpose of this group activity is to give students a better understanding of the people who work at school, their jobs, their work locations, and their personal interests.

It would be helpful to make and laminate a large map of the school building and its surrounding area. You may prefer to put photographs of the school workers at their work locations. The map would aid the students all year in routing them to various school locations, such as fire exit routes, office routes, playground routes, and so on.

Arrange to visit the people who work at school at their job locations or invite them to your classroom. You may want to give groups of students the responsibility of arranging the workers' visits. Many communication skills could be used: written or oral invitations, conducting interviews, thank you notes, and so on.

The following ideas could be used in the interviews:

What do you do at school?

What training did you need?

How did you get this job?

What do you like best about your job?

What don't you like about your job?

What other kinds of jobs have you had?

How do you get to school?

Do you have any hobbies?

Where were you born?

Where do you live?

What is your favorite color?

What is your favorite book or movie?

What is your favorite television show?

Where in the world would you like to travel? Why?

"SCHOOL" HOME ACTIVITY ENRICHMENT PAGE

Return by _____

Date _____

Dear Parent,

We will be finding out more about our school in our Social Studies unit.

Many of our students are unaware of the changes in schools and curriculums that have taken place since you or your parents were in elementary school.

Please help your child gain a better understanding of your school experiences by answering any questions he or she might have including the following:

1. What was the name of your elementary school? _____

2. How did you get to school? _____

3. Who were two of your teachers? _____

4. What subject did you like best? _____

5. What subject didn't you like? _____

6. Did you have recess? _____

7. What games did you like to play? _____

8. Did you have Music, Physical Education, or Art Teachers? _____
_____

9. What rules did you have at school? _____
_____

10. Who were your two best friends? _____

I would also welcome any Grandparent interviews that could be arranged. Please feel free to add any additional comment pages and return with this page by _____.

Thank you for your continued support.

Sincerely,

Your child's teacher

I've learned about schools old and new.

name _____

Home Activity Award

_____'s

work is
really sharp !

School Award

Chalk Talk!

_____

_____

_____

_____

_____

Congratulations! _____ 19__

PAY TO THE
ORDER OF _____ for outstanding
work at school today.
This award may be used
for_____

_____

teacher's signature

School Awards

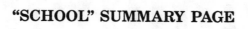

"SCHOOL" SUMMARY PAGE

Name _____ Date _____

1. What is the name of our school? _____

2. When was our school built? _____

3. Who is our principal? _____

4. What time does our school day begin? _____

5. What time do we go out for recess? _____

6. What time do we go to Lunch? _____

7. What time do we go home? _____

8. How can you help a substitute teacher? _____

_____

9. What are three school rules? _____

_____

_____

10. List the five school days of the week and any special activities for each day:

Day	Special Activity
1. _____	_____
2. _____	_____
3. _____	_____
4. _____	_____
5. _____	_____

11. List eight things that you use in our classroom:

1. _____ 2. _____

3. _____ 4. _____

5. _____ 6. _____

7. _____ 8. _____

Community

Welcome to

_____

population : _____

1   8

2   7

3   4   5   6

Center Marker

"COMMUNITY" CENTER MARKER

A learning center marker is provided for students using the Social Studies unit at learning centers. (Refer to page 230.)

Distribute copies of the billboard marker to the students. The students can fill the name and the population of their town on the markers, cut out their markers, and place them near the "Community" Learning Centers.

"COMMUNITY" DISCOVERIES

Date _____

Dear Parent,

During the next two weeks our Social Studies unit will be about our community. Your child will gain a better understanding of our community.

Our class map skill activity will feature a floor map of our community. Your child will create buildings and natural features for the map.

Please send several coupons from magazines and newspapers that would be appropriate for our class to use at a Coupon Clippers center.

Your child will make a telephone directory. He or she will need to know his or her telephone number. If your telephone number is unlisted, it will *not* be written in our directory. However, please be sure that your child knows it in the event that he or she would need it. You may want to review your family's rules for telephone usage.

Safety will be emphasized at our Signs for Safety Center. Your child will make a pennant which he or she will want to display at home. If you have any heavy fabric remnants which measure at least 10″ × 24″ such as felt, discarded window shades, and so on, please send them.

Your child will need an empty shoe box or facial tissue box to make a diorama of a community helper.

Please send coupons, fabric remnants, and an empty shoe box or facial tissue box by _____.

You are welcome to visit us and see our centers in action. Please contact me for a convenient time.

Thank you for your continued support.

Sincerely,

Your child's teacher

Date _____

From Home
To School

Dear _____,

_____
_____
_____
_____
_____
_____
_____
_____
_____
_____
_____
_____
_____
_____
_____
_____
_____

_____
Parent Signature

Dear Parent,

     I would appreciate any feedback you or your child may have regarding the "Community" Social Studies activities: Our Community, My Neighbor, Signs for Safety, Coupon Clippers, Community News, My Shopping Trip, Community Helpers, and My Telephone Directory.

     Please use this page for comments and return it to me by _____

_____.

                              Sincerely,

                              Your child's teacher

"COMMUNITY" LEARNING CENTERS LIST

These activities focus on various aspects of the community.

"Our Community" Center

(Bulletin board is used with this activity.)

Content areas: Social studies, communication, motor

Skills: Mapping, classifying, creating, coordination, using references, matching

Activities:

1. Sort and tack feature cards under the corresponding photographs.
2. Make a building and a natural feature for the floor map.

"Signs for Safety" Center

Content areas: Social studies, motor

Skills: Classifying, coordination, creating, matching

Activities:

1. Match the signs to the words on the student activity page.
2. Make a safety pennant.

"Coupon Clippers" Center

Content areas: Math, motor, social studies

Skills: Money values, coordination, problem solving, comparing

Activities:

1. Make a coupon game.
2. Add the value of the coupons on a calculator or adding machine.

"Community News" Center

(Open-ended activity)

Content areas: Social studies, communication, motor, teacher's choice

Skills: Using references, classifying, coordination, teacher's choice

Activities:

1. Read the newspaper.
2. Cut out and paste stories and ads onto paper.

"My Neighbor" Center

Content areas: Communication, motor

Skills: Listening, creating, creative writing

Activities:

1. Listen to the cassette tape of the book.
2. Make a puppet.

"My Telephone Directory" Center

Content areas: Social studies, motor

Skills: Classifying, using references, handwriting, self-image, spelling

Activities:

1. Look for your telephone number in the telephone directory.
2. Make a telephone directory.

"My Shopping Trip" Center

Content areas: Social studies, communication, motor

Skills: Classifying, vocabulary development, using references, handwriting, coordination

Activities:

1. Draw stores on three bags.
2. Write the words for each store category.

"Community Helpers" Center

Content areas: Social studies, motor

Skills: Using references, creating, coordination

Activities:

1. Look at books and select one community helper for a diorama.
2. Make a diorama.

TEACHER'S DIRECTIONS FOR "OUR COMMUNITY" CENTER

Content areas: Social studies, communication, motor

Skills: Mapping, classifying, creating, coordination, using references, matching

Materials needed:

> Bulletin board
> One block of scrap wood per student (source: parents, lumber yard, sawmill). The size of the wood will be determined by the teacher depending on the map scale (refer to "Materials preparation" below)
> One piece of sandpaper per student
> A supply of newspaper
> An assortment of permanent marking pens
> An assortment of construction paper
> Scissors
> Paste
> Thumbtacks and a container for them
> Teacher-made set of feature photographs and word cards
> An envelope for the word cards

Materials preparation:

1. Schedule a field trip a few weeks prior to beginning the Community Social Studies unit to familiarize the students with the various important features and streets of your community. Photograph the natural features such as streams, rivers, rocks, hills, woods, as well as man-made features (community buildings). (Two weeks should allow ample time for film development.) If a field trip is impossible, you or a few parents can photograph the above features. Another option would be to have your students draw pictures of the above features.

2. Prepare an "Our Community" bulletin board as pictured on the file folder directions page. Mount the man-made feature photographs on yellow construction paper and the natural features on green construction paper. Make a set of feature word cards using 3″ by 5″ index cards and a black water-base marking pen. To make the card activity self-checking you may want to number the photographs and write the corresponding number on the back of the word cards. (You may want to color code the cards for the younger student by placing a yellow dot on

the man-made feature cards and a green dot on the natural feature cards.) Laminate the cards and an envelope for them.

3. Make a floor map of your community from durable plastic, paper, or fabric (you determine the size). Draw streets, bridges, railroad tracks, and so on. Place the floor map under the "Our Community" bulletin board.

4. You will need to determine the number of buildings that you want the students to make for the floor map. Provide a checklist with the names of the buildings listed vertically on it. Leave space for the student to sign his or her name next to the building name when he or she has completed it.

DIRECTIONS FOR FILE FOLDER ACTIVITIES:

Activity 1

The student tacks the feature cards under the corresponding photographs on the bulletin board.

Activity 2

The student makes a building and a natural feature for the floor map referring to the bulletin board pictures.

1. He or she looks at the checklist and chooses a building that has not been completed.
2. The student sandpapers a block of wood over newspaper.
3. Then he or she uses marking pens to design the building, write the building name and his or her initials on the bottom of the wood.
4. Next the student makes a natural feature using assorted construction paper, scissors, paste, and marking pens.
5. He or she places the building and the natural feature on the map.
6. The student signs his or her name on the checklist.

Thinking it over:

Discussion questions:

1. What are some man-made features of our community?
2. What are some natural features?
3. Where is the fire department located?
4. Where is the post office located?
5. Where is the school located?
6. Where is the police department located?

One step beyond activities:

1. Make copies of your community map or obtain maps from your Chamber of Commerce. Either give written or oral directions for the following map activities:

   a. Put a red "x" on your house.
   b. Draw a green line from your house to our school.
   c. Draw a blue line from our school to the fire department.
   d. Draw an orange line from the fire department to the library.
   e. Draw a purple line from the library to the post office.
Continue with other directions which are appropriate for your area.

2. You and the students make a list of all the facilities that a town could have: post office, bus station, train station, airport, library, hospital, shopping center, newspaper office, bank, radio station, television station, swimming pool, park, zoo, playground, and so on. Discuss and circle the ones that exist in your town. How far away is the nearest one?

Our Community

1 Match the cards to the pictures.

Our Community
has people-made and natural features.

park

river

Cards

2 Make a building.
Make a natural feature.

Now put them
on the map.

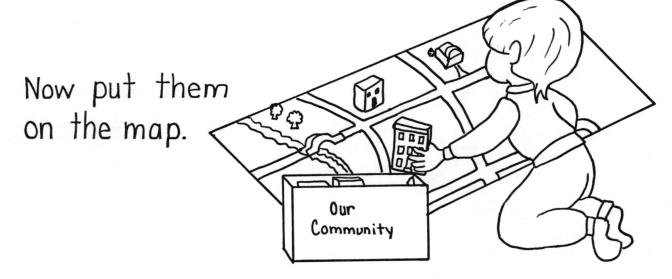

Our
Community

File Folder Directions

TEACHER'S DIRECTIONS FOR "SIGNS FOR SAFETY" CENTER

Content areas: Social studies, motor

Skills: Classifying, coordination, creating

Materials needed:

> Copies of student activity page
> One 24″ by 10″ strip of fabric remnant (felt, discarded window shades, and so on) per student
> Yellow and white construction paper squares, 4 inches or larger
> Red and black marking pens
> Scissors (suitable for cutting fabric)
> Stapler and staples
> Teacher-made posterboard pennant and signs patterns
> Teacher-made signs chart
> Pencil
> Crayons

Materials preparation:

1. Discuss traffic signs in your community, such as kinds, shapes, purpose, colors, meanings, and so on. You may want to refer to books such as Hoban, Tana, *I Read Signs,* Greenwillow Books, New York, 1983; Maestro, Betsy and Guilio, *Harriet Reads Signs and More Signs,* Crown Publishing, New York, 1980.
   You also may obtain sign information from your state department of transportation.
2. Make an example signs chart by using a student activity page.
3. Make posterboard patterns of a pennant (cut a triangle shape to fit the 24″ by 10″ fabric) and the five signs (approximately 3″ in diameter) as shown on the file folder direction page.
4. You may wish to suggest ways to hang the pennant, such as staple to a coat hanger, yardstick, or dowel.

DIRECTIONS FOR FILE FOLDER ACTIVITIES:

Activity 1

The student matches the signs to the words on the student activity page with a pencil. The student colors the signs on the student page referring to books or your example chart.

Activity 2

The student makes a safety pennant:
1. He or she traces your triangular pattern onto fabric with a pencil or marking pen, then cuts it out.
2. The student uses a pencil to trace your sign patterns onto yellow and white construction paper, then cuts them out.
3. He or she uses the marking pens to make the appropriate symbols on the signs referring to your chart.
4. The student staples the signs onto the triangular fabric.

Thinking it over:

Discussion questions:

1. How do you keep safe in your neighborhood?
2. How many people walk to school?
3. Who taught you how to walk from home to school?
4. Where do you cross streets?
5. Are there any signs or people that help you cross streets safely?
6. How many people ride a bus to school?
7. What signs are helpful to your bus driver?
8. Does anyone cross a railroad track on the way to school?
9. What rules do you know about railroad tracks?

One step beyond activities:

1. Take a walking field trip near your school to observe safety signs. When you return to school draw signs on the chalkboard. Discuss where the signs are found and what they mean.
2. Invite a police officer to talk to the class about pedestrian and bicycle safety. As a follow-up activity the students can make posters depicting pedestrian and bicycle safety.

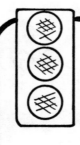 

Signs for Safety

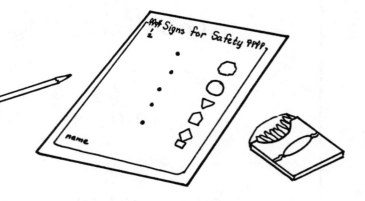

1 Do the ditto.

2 Make a safety pennant.

File Folder Directions

Signs for Safety

1. Draw lines to match the words and signs.
2. Color the signs correctly.

school crossing •

yield •

bike crossing •
(possible hazard)

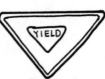

stop •

railroad crossing •

name _____

Student Activity Page

TEACHER'S DIRECTIONS FOR "COUPON CLIPPERS" CENTER

Content areas: Math, motor

Skills: Money values, coordination, problem solving, sorting

Materials needed:

> A collection of coupons (refer to parent letter)
> Eight 5" by 7" index cards per student
> One 4" by 9½" envelope per student
> Paste
> Scissors
> Pencil
> Calculator or adding machine
> A collection of coins: penny, nickel, dime, quarter
> *Options:* a coin stamp set and ink pad

Materials preparation:

1. You will need to determine the difficulty of this activity by controlling the money value of selected coupons from the collection.
2. Make sure your students know how to use a calculator or an adding machine to total the value of their coupon savings.

DIRECTIONS FOR FILE FOLDER ACTIVITIES:

Activity 1

The student chooses eight coupons from the collection. He or she pastes a coupon onto the top half of each of eight index cards as pictured on the file folder directions. He or she traces coins, makes coin rubbings, or uses a coin stamp set to show the value of the coupon on the bottom half of the index cards. Then the student cuts each card apart differently to make the game self-checking.

Activity 2

The student adds the value of the eight coupons on an adding machine or a calculator. He or she writes his or her name and the total coupon savings amount on the outside of the envelope.

Thinking it over:

Discussion questions:

1. Does your family use coupons at stores?
2. Why do people use coupons?
3. Why do businesses offer coupons?
4. Where can you find coupons?
5. Where does your family keep coupons?
6. Do you help sort the coupons? How do you group them?
7. Why do many coupons have a date on them?
8. What does an expiration date mean?

One step beyond activities:

1. Use the coupon collection. Divide the class into small groups for the following classifying activities:

   Group 1: Use yellow marking pens to underline the expiration dates. Then sort the coupons by the months of expiration dates.
   Group 2: Sort coupons into categories such as meat, dairy, baking products, cleaning products, paper products, and so on.
   Group 3: Sort coupons in alphabetical order by product names.
   Group 4: Sort coupons into price discount value categories.

2. Conduct a shopping survey. Ask the students to choose their favorite grocery store from two or three stores. Let the students list the reasons for their choices, such as double coupon days, lower prices, better ads, free samples, and so on. Make a comparison graph of the survey results.

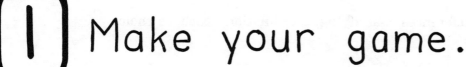

Coupon Clippers

1 Make your game.

2 Add the value of your coupons.

File Folder Directions

TEACHER'S DIRECTIONS FOR "COMMUNITY NEWS" CENTER

(Open-ended activity)

Content areas: Social studies, communication, motor, teacher's choice

Skills: Using references, classifying, coordination, teacher's choice

Materials needed:

> Copies of different editions of your community newspaper (one per student)
> Pencil
> Scissors
> Paste
> Crayons
> Paper

Materials preparation:

The focus of this activity is to familiarize students with their community newspaper. Emphasis should also be placed on the role the newspaper plays as a source of communicating information.

Due to the wide range of variances in communities, newspapers, and student ability levels, you will need to determine the following things for this activity:

1. The size and number of pages for the student's papers.
2. The kinds of skills you wish to teach.
3. The kinds of articles you want to emphasize such as news, sports, comics, weather, classified ads, and so on.

Some ideas which may be used with younger students are:

1. Cut out the weather news. "What do you think the weather will be tomorrow?" Draw a picture about it.
2. Cut out an animal story. Underline with a green crayon all of the words that start like monkey. Underline with a red crayon all of the words that start like lion.

3. Cut out movie ads of shows you have seen or would like to see.

4. Cut apart a cartoon strip. Then paste the story in the order that it happened (1, 2, 3, 4, 5, 6, and so on).

5. Find a story about school. Cut out ten words and paste them in alphabetical order.

6. Cut out a grocery store ad. Circle all of the 5's with a green crayon, all of the 9's with a blue crayon. How many 5's are there in your ad? How many 9's?

7. Cut out one of your favorite restaurant ads. Draw pictures of the foods you like to eat there.

Some ideas for older students are:

1. Cut out and paste 10 different statistics about your community.

2. Make your own community cartoon strip.

3. Circle the names of five places you have never heard of in the news section. Find these places on a map.

4. Cut out six abbreviations in the classified ads and paste them on your paper. Write the abbreviation meanings. Write an ad to sell something your mother wants you to get rid of.

5. Cut out 6 stories in the newspaper. Carefully cut off and save the headlines and the stories. Mix up the headlines on your desk, then try matching the correct headline with it's story.

6. Choose your favorite sport. Find the sports page and cut-out any words that are about that sport. Paste the words in a sports jacket outline on your paper.

7. Cut out and paste the name of the newspaper, cost, name of editor, and name of publisher. Write a letter to the editor about something you would like to see changed in your community.

For additional ideas please contact the editor of your newspaper. Many major newspapers sponsor newspaper in education programs.

DIRECTIONS FOR FILE FOLDER ACTIVITIES:

Activity 1

The student reads the newspaper.

Activity 2

The student cuts out stories and ads, and pastes them on his or her paper as per teacher directions.

Thinking it over:

Discussion questions:

1. What newspaper is published in our community?
2. How often is it published?
3. How much does it cost?
4. Does your family subscribe to a newspaper?
5. How does the paper get to your home?
6. Are there paper boys and girls who deliver papers in your town?
7. Do any of you have a newspaper route? Would you like to?
8. How much money do paper boys and girls make in one week?
9. What can you learn from a newspaper that you can't learn by watching T.V.?
10. What is your favorite section of the newspaper?

One step beyond activities:

1. Make a class newspaper or newsletter. Divide the students into small groups with each group being responsible for specific parts. You may want to recruit parents or aides to help younger students with this project. The younger students could dictate the stories for the parents to type. You may want to include a section on riddles/jokes, new library books, student birthdays, best spellers, perfect attendance students, and so on.
2. Make a class chart or graph of "Ways to Communicate in Our Town." Compare ways to communicate such as television, radio, newspapers, with communication methods used 50 years ago in your town.

Community News

1 Read the newspaper.

2 Cut out stories and ads. Paste them on paper.

File Folder Directions

TEACHER'S DIRECTIONS FOR "MY NEIGHBOR" CENTER

Content areas: Communication, motor

Skills: Listening, creating, creative writing

Materials needed:

> A collection of scrap materials, such as cardboard strips, yarn, crepe paper, paper plates, paper bags, assorted colors and sizes of construction paper.
> Glue
> Scissors
> Pencil
> Crayons
> Masking tape
> Stapler and staples
> Tape recorder
> Cassette tape
> A book about neighborhoods such as Hughes, Shirley, *Alfie Gets in First*, Lothrop, Lee and Shepard Books, New York, 1981; Rogers, Fred, *Moving*, G. P. Putnam's Sons, New York, 1987.

Materials preparation:

- Prepare a cassette tape of the book you have chosen.
- Discuss neighbors (people and pets), ways to share, and interdependence.

DIRECTIONS FOR FILE FOLDER ACTIVITIES:

Activity 1

The student listens to the cassette tape of the book.

Activity 2

The student uses scrap materials to make a puppet depicting "My Neighbor."

Optional activity:

The student may write a story about the neighbor he or she depicted.

Thinking it over:

Discussion questions:

1. Who lives in your neighborhood?
2. Where can you play in your neighborhood?
3. Who do you play with?
4. What family do you like to visit in your neighborhood? Why?
5. How do the families in your neighborhood help each other?
6. Have you ever moved?
7. How did you meet the kids in your new neighborhood?

One step beyond activities:

1. Encourage the students to accompany a family member on a visit to a neighbor (preferably a new one). They could find out the following kinds of information about the neighbor: "What do you like to do for fun?" "What are some of your favorite things?" "Do you like to collect certain things?" "Do you have any pets?" "What jobs do you like to do at home and away from your home?" "Do you have anything I could help you do?" You may want to have the students discuss the information with the class.
2. Creative writing. Some ideas are:

   a. If I could move to a new neighborhood, I would _____.
   b. One time my next-door neighbors helped me _____.
   c. If I could change something in my neighborhood I would ____.
   d. I think it would be great if a whole group of my neighbors _
   _____.

My Neighbor

1  Listen to the book.

2 Make a puppet of your neighbor.

Things for Puppets

paper, markers, sticks, plates, bags, yarn, buttons, fabric

bag

plate

File Folder Directions

TEACHER'S DIRECTIONS FOR "MY TELEPHONE DIRECTORY" CENTER

Content areas: Social studies, motor

Skills: Classifying, using references, handwriting, self-image, spelling

Materials needed:

> Copies of student activity page
> Pencil
> Crayons
> Telephone directory
> Seven 8½ by 11 inch pieces of newsprint or ruled notebook paper per student
> Stapler and staples
> Teacher-made telephone directory

Materials preparation:

1. Make an alphabetized telephone directory. Fold and staple seven pieces of paper inside a folded student activity page cover. Write the letters of the alphabet in order on the pages. *Optional:* you may want to staple books for younger students.
2. Make an alphabetized class list for the students to copy.
3. Provide a telephone directory of your community. You may want to highlight the names of your students' families with a marking pen.
4. Discuss the rules for proper telephone usage. A toy telephone may be used by the students to practice calls.

DIRECTIONS FOR FILE FOLDER ACTIVITIES:

Activity 1

The student will look for his or her telephone number in the telephone directory of the community.

Activity 2

The student makes a telephone directory as per your example. He or she copies the alphabetized class list and writes the telephone numbers using the community telephone directory as a reference. (You may want the younger student to only find 6 of his or her friends' telephone numbers; then complete the others at home. You would need to make copies of the class list for the students.)

Thinking it over:

Discussion questions:

1. Do you know who invented the telephone? (Alexander Graham Bell)
2. Do you know when it was invented? (1876)
3. How many telephones do you have?
4. Do you have any rules about using the telephone at home?
5. Do you know the emergency telephone numbers to call for the police department, fire department, and ambulance?
6. Do your parents leave a list of telephone numbers for the baby sitter to use at your house?
7. Did your parents give our school office their telephone numbers at home and at work?
8. Did your parents give the name and telephone number of a person who could help you if they cannot be reached?

One step beyond activities:

1. Collect a set of outdated telephone directories. (Ask parents to send in their old directories when they receive new ones.) You may want to have your students try some of the following ideas:

    a. List people whose last names are colors.
    b. List people who have the same first name as yours.

    c. List people who live on your street.

    d. List people with four or less letters in their last name.

    e. List the telephone numbers of the fire department and the police department.

You may want to make copies of some telephone directory pages for younger students to use. These students could circle the requested information on the pages instead of listing them.

2. Play "Beat the Clock." After the students have completed several telephone directory assignments independently, try dividing them into small groups (3–5 students). Each student will need a telephone directory. Give a telephone directory assignment to the entire class, set a timer for a specific time the group who finishes the assignment in the required time wins. (The information will be shared orally.)

3. Compare out-of-town telephone directories with your own community's directory. Encourage out-of-town relatives and friends to donate them. If your library has out-of-town directories, you may want to have your students go there to make comparisons.

My Telephone Directory

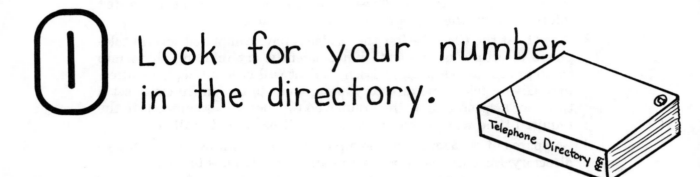

1 Look for your number in the directory.

2 Make a directory.

File Folder Directions

My Telephone Directory

my name

Emergency Numbers:

Fire _____

Police_____

Mom at work:

_____

Neighbors:

_____

_____

_____

Student Activity Page

TEACHER'S DIRECTIONS FOR "MY SHOPPING TRIP" CENTER

Content areas: Social studies, communication, motor

Skills: Classifying, vocabulary development, using references, handwriting, co-ordination

Materials needed:

> Three 5½ by 10½ inch bags per student
> Crayons
> Pencil
> Paper (approximately 2 by 2 inch)
> References: dictionary–pictionary

Materials preparation:

1. Determine the number of words you want the student to write for each category, clothes, food, toys.
2. You may want to make three stores on the bags as pictured on the file folder directions page.

DIRECTIONS FOR FILE FOLDER ACTIVITIES:

Activity 1

The student draws a store on each of three bags as pictured on the file folder directions page.

Activity 2

Using references the student writes the words for each store category on paper. He or she sorts the words into the bags. He or she may draw pictures on the opposite side of the paper.

Thinking it over:

Discussion questions:

1. Who does the shopping in your family?
2. Where does your family shop for food? Toys? Clothes?
3. Does your family buy anything from catalogs?
4. What do you help buy?
5. Do you have your own money to spend?
6. How do you get money?

One step beyond activities:

1. Make "My Family Shopper's Guides." Each student will need three sheets of notebook paper and a telephone directory. He or she heads the sheets "Foods, Clothes, Toys." Then using the yellow pages of the telephone directory, the student lists the names, addresses, and telephone numbers of the stores where his or her family shops for the items.
2. "Let's Go Shopping!" Game. Write the letters of the alphabet on the chalkboard. Invite the students to go on a "shopping trip." (You choose a category: toys, food, or clothes.) You call out a student's name and point to one letter of the alphabet. The student must name something beginning with that letter that he or she could buy in a "Toy" store. When he or she responds correctly, erase the letter. Continue to call out the students' names and alphabet letters in random order until there are no letters remaining on the chalkboard. Then you may want to play the game again featuring another category such as "Food."

My Shopping Trip

1 Make a store on each bag.

   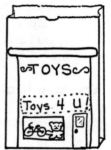

2 Write the words.

File Folder Directions

TEACHER'S DIRECTIONS FOR "COMMUNITY HELPERS" CENTER

Content areas: Social studies, motor

Skills: Using references, creating, coordination

Materials needed:

> One shoe box or facial tissue paper box per student
> Marking pens
> Crayons
> Scissors
> Paste
> An assortment of construction paper
> Books about community helpers such as Brill, Marlene Targ, *I Can be a Lawyer,* Childrens Press, Chicago, 1987; Behrens, June, *I Can Be a Nurse,* Childrens Press, Chicago, 1986; Hankin, Rebecca, *I Can be a Fire Fighter,* Childrens Press, Chicago, 1985; Lillegard, Dee, *I Can Be a Baker,* Children's Press, Chicago, 1986; Lumley, Kay, *I Can Be an Animal Doctor,* Childrens Press, Chicago, 1985; Matthias, Catherine, *I Can Be a Police Officer,* Childrens Press, Chicago, 1984.

Materials preparation:

1. Establish background information about community helpers by using audio-visual aids, books, and so on.
2. You may want to make an example diorama in a shoe box with background and a community helper in it.

DIRECTIONS FOR FILE FOLDER ACTIVITIES:

Activity 1

The student looks at books and selects one community helper for his or her diorama.

Activity 2

The student uses marking pens, construction paper, and a box to create a diorama of a community helper.

Optional activity

The student can write a story about the community helper in his or her diorama.

Thinking it over:

Discussion questions:

1. If you went to a restaurant, who would take your order?
2. If you wanted to buy postage stamps, who would help you?
3. If you wanted to buy a special birthday cake, where could you go to order one? Who would help you?
4. If your dog was sick, who would you call to help him?
5. If you wanted to put money in a savings account, who would you see?
6. If your house was on fire, who would you call?

One step beyond activities:

1. Arrange to have parents or other people from your community talk to the students about their occupations. Schedule their visits over a one- to two-week time span. Encourage them to wear the clothes they wear to work. They might also bring any equipment they use on their job. Ask the people to emphasize the job preparations which they needed before they were hired.
2. The students can use career reference books, pictionaries, and dictionaries. The students can list or draw pictures of the community workers who help them stay healthy, keep them safe, and so on.

Community Helpers

1 Look at books.

2 Make a diorama about a helper.

File Folder Directions

TEACHER'S DIRECTIONS FOR "COMMUNITY" ENRICHMENT CENTERS

"Community" Group Activity

Community speakers, local community trips, "Anti-Litter" project, "Neighborhood Clean-Up Day".

"Community" Home Activity

Duplicate the pages on colored paper. Send the pages home one week prior to beginning the Community Social Studies unit. You may want to modify the Community Trivia page depending on your area.

"Community" Awards

Duplicate the pages on colored paper. Give each child who returns the "Community" Home Activity a Home Activity Award. The other "Community" Awards may be used for the recognition of good work, and so on.

"Community" Summary Activity

You may duplicate the Community Summary page for older students to complete independently. You may use the page for discussion questions with younger students.

"COMMUNITY" GROUP ACTIVITIES

As a culminating activity to the community social studies unit you may want to try one or more of the following ideas:

1. *Tour a local museum* if there is one available, to find out more about your community past and present.

2. *Invite a person from a local historical society to talk to your class* and give an audiovisual presentation about the history of your community.

3. *Invite senior citizens to talk to your class about the changes that have taken place in your community in the past 40 to 50 years.*

4. *Invite the mayor or other government officials to discuss their jobs and community rules.*

5. *Organize an "Anti-Litter" week at school.* Plan a walk to collect litter in an area near your school. Give each student a bag to collect litter. When you return to school, let the students sort their litter, then decorate "Anti-Litter" posters with the junk. Display the posters throughout your school.

6. *Organize a "Neighborhood Clean-up Day".* Recruit parents to help. Write a letter to the editor of your newspaper for help in advertising this project. Emphasis could be placed on sorting and recycling discarded materials.

7. *Play Community Trivia riddles.* You or the students make up several 3" × 5" index cards with riddles about your community written on them. The riddle information may be taken from the Community Trivia page. The students can take turns answering them.

8. *Make arrangements for your students to exchange letters with students who live in a community that is very different from yours.* You may do this as a class project. Your students could describe your community, send pictures of your area, enclose your community newspaper, and so on. Your students may want to continue on a pen pal basis with the other students.

**COMMUNITY HOME ACTIVITY
ENRICHMENT PAGE**

RETURN BY _____ **DATE** _____

Dear Parent,

Next week we will begin a Social Studies unit about our community. The purpose will be to encourage your child to become more aware of our community and its people.

Please help your child find out the "Community Trivia" information on the attached page. Feel free to add any extra comments or data you may find. Please return the information by _____.

Some sources of information may be the Chamber of Commerce, the reference librarian, the Mayor or local government offices, museum, historical society, senior citizen groups, and other people in our community.

Thank you for your help with this Community Trivia activity. I am sure that both you and your child will gain new insights about our community.

Sincerely,

Your child's teacher

"COMMUNITY" TRIVIA

Name _____

Return by _____

1. When was our community first settled? _____

2. What was the population then? _____

3. Who were the first settlers? _____

4. Why did they decide to settle here? _____
_____
_____

5. Where were three of the first businesses established in our community?
_____
_____

6. When was the first school built? _____ Where? _____
_____ Name? _____

7. What is the oldest existing church? _____
When was it built? _____

8. Who has the oldest tombstone in the _____ cemetery?
_____ Date? _____

9. What is the tallest structure? _____

10. What year were the first records kept about our community?
_____

11. Who was the first mayor? _____

12. Who is the mayor now? _____

13. Who is the fire chief? _____

14. Who is the police chief? _____ , _____

15. What is our current population? _____

16. What is our elevation? _____

17. Where was the first Post Office located? _____

18. Where was the first Library? _____

19. Where was the first Fire Station? _____

20. Where was the first Police Station? _____

I'm a master
of
Community Trivia.

_____

Home Activity Award

Community Award

Stop! Look! Listen!

_____ is on
the right track!

As these papers
clearly show,
I really know
the

WAY TO GO!

name _____

Community Awards

"COMMUNITY" SUMMARY PAGE

Name _____ Date _____

1. What is the name of our community? _____

2. What year was our community founded? _____

3. What is the population of our community? _____

4. Draw four community safety signs:

    _____ _____ _____ _____

5. Why do people use coupons? _____

6. What is the name of our community's newspaper? _____
   _____ How much does it cost? _____

7. Who is one of your neighbors? _____

8. List the telephone numbers for: you _____
   police _____, fire dept. _____

9. If you had money to go shopping, make a list of the items you would
   buy: Food: 1. _____ 2. _____
        Clothes: 1. _____ 2. _____
        Toys: 1. _____ 2. _____ _____

10. List four people in our community who help you: _____
    _____

    _____

11. Where is our school located? _____

    _____

State

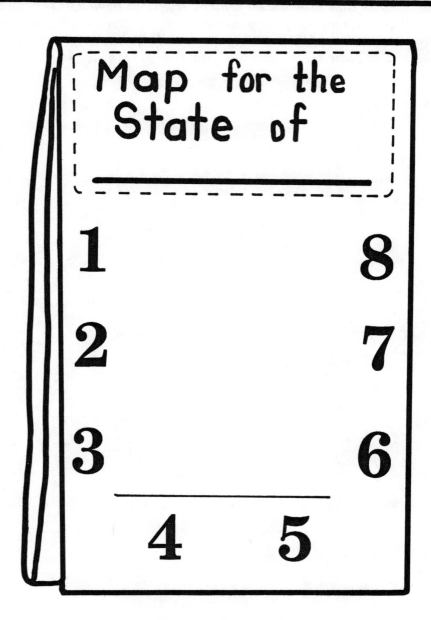

Map for the
State of
_____

1   8

2   7

3   6

_____

4   5

Center Marker

"STATE" CENTER MARKER

A learning center marker is provided for students using the Social Studies unit at learning centers. (Refer to page 230.)

Distribute copies of the map marker to the students. The students can draw an outline of their state in the middle of their map, cut out their markers, and place them near the "State" Learning Centers.

OUR GREAT STATE

Date _____

Dear Parent,

 During the next two weeks our Social Studies unit will feature activities about our state.

 The bulletin board will display the United States map, our state map, and our community map. Your child will gain a better understanding of where he or she lives. Emphasis will be placed on comparing the size and shape of our state with other states, locating our capital, recognizing abbreviations, and so on. You may wish to extend these map skill activities at home.

 Our state symbol learning centers will include the flag, bird, tree, and flower. Additional wildlife common to our state will be studied.

 Your child will have an opportunity to use a typewriter at our state potpourri center. He or she will type an ingredients label for his or her potpourri bag. You may want to let your child use a typewriter at home also.

 Anticipate receiving a long strip of post cards with information about our state. Encourage your child to mail the post cards and the state potpourri bag to friends or relatives who live out of state.

 You may want to help your child learn more facts about our state such as our motto, nickname, abbreviation, names of some of our state officials, and so on.

 Thank you for your support.

Sincerely,

Your child's teacher

Date _____

Dear _____,

_____
_____
_____
_____
_____
_____
_____
_____
_____
_____
_____
_____
_____
_____
_____
_____
_____

_____
Parent Signature

Dear Parent,

I would appreciate any feedback you or your child may have regarding the "State" Social Studies activities: Where is My State, My State Flag, My State Flower, My State Tree, State Wildlife, My State Bird, State Potpourri, Greetings! From My State.

Please use this page for comments and return it to me by _____.

Sincerely,

Your child's teacher

"STATE" LEARNING CENTERS LIST

These activities emphasize state symbols, features, products, and locations.

"Where Is My State" Center

(Bulletin board is used with this activity.)

Content areas: Social studies, motor

Skills: Mapping, classifying, comparing, using references, coordination

Activities:

1. Locate your state on the U.S. map.
   Complete information on the student activity page.
2. Make a state map pin design.

"My State Flag" Center

Content areas: Social studies, communication, motor

Skills: Using references, creating, creative writing, coordination

Activities:

1. Make the state flag.
2. Write about the state flag.

"My State Flower" Center

Content areas: Social studies, communication, motor

Skills: Classifying, creative writing, creating, coordination, using references

Activities:

1. Make the state flower.
2. Write about the state flower.

"My State Tree" Puzzle Center

(Open-ended activity)

Content areas: Social studies, motor, teacher's choice

Skills: Classifying, creating, coordination, teacher's choice

Activities:

1. Write the information on the student activity page.
2. Draw the state tree and make the puzzle.

"State Wildlife" Center

Content areas: Social studies, communication, motor

Skills: Using references, listening, creating

Activities:

1. Listen to the cassette tape of the book.
2. Paint a wildlife picture.

"My State Bird" Center

Content areas: Social studies, communication, motor

Skills: Classifying, comparing, creating, coordination, using references, handwriting

Activities:

1. Make the state bird.
2. Compare other state birds.

"State Potpourri" Center

Content areas: Social studies, communication, motor

Skills: Classifying, sorting, coordination, using references, spelling, vocabulary development

Activities:

1. Choose eight objects from the potpourri collection.
2. Type the names of the objects on the label.

"Greetings! From My State" Center

Content areas: Social studies, communication, motor

Skills: Classifying, handwriting, using references, creating, coordination

Activities:

1. Make the post cards.
2. Paste the post cards onto the strip.

TEACHER'S DIRECTIONS FOR "WHERE IS MY STATE?" CENTER

Content areas: Social studies, motor

Skills: Mapping, classifying, comparing, using references, coordination

Materials needed:

Bulletin board
Copies of student activity page
Copies of teacher-made state map outline paper
9″ × 12″ construction paper (one per student)
Straight pins
Stapler and staples
Pencil
Crayons
Carpet sample
Maps of the United States, your state, your community

Materials preparation:

1. Prepare a bulletin board as shown here:

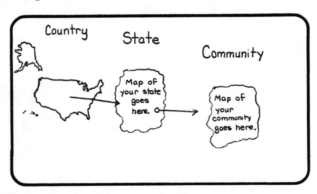

2. Establish necessary background information about the maps on the bulletin board to show comparisons between country, state, and community. Review cardinal directions: North, South, East, and West.
3. Make an outline map of your state on 8½″ × 11″ paper. Write the name of your community and state capital. Place a dot at each of those locations. Make copies of the map (one per student) to use for pin designs.
4. Prepare the outline map paper in the following way for a pin design: Place the outline map paper on top of a piece of construction paper. Staple the corners of both papers together. Insert a straight pin through the top of the outline map paper.
5. Provide a carpet sample at this area to protect the desk top from pin scratches.

DIRECTIONS FOR FILE FOLDER ACTIVITIES:

Activity 1

The student locates his or her state on the United States map on the bulletin board. Then he or she completes the information on the student activity page including the cardinal directions.

Activity 2

The student makes a state pin design.

1. He or she removes the straight pin from the top of the outline map paper.
2. He or she uses the pin to punch holes through the outline of the map and the dots indicating the capital and community locations. (Be sure the student does this work over the carpet sample.)
3. He or she removes the outline map paper from the construction paper. (The outline of the state map will be visible on the construction paper.)

Thinking it over:

Discussion questions:

1. What states, countries, or bodies of water border our state on the north, south, east, and west?
2. Where is our state capital?
3. Has that city always been our state capital?
4. What size is our state compared to other states?
5. What shape is our state compared to other states?
6. Can you find six cities on the state map that start with "C"?
7. Can you trace the route from your home to school on the community map?
8. Can you trace the shortest route from school to the Post Office?

One step beyond activities:

1. Puzzles. Use the United States map puzzle to help students compare state sizes, learn capitals, geographic locations, and so on. Use the state map puzzle to find out information about your state. (If state map puzzles are not available for your state, the students could make them by mounting state maps on posterboard and cutting them apart.)

2. Make a license plate class book. Each student can copy his or her license plate on a page. Then have the students write the letters of the alphabet vertically on the notebook paper. They can become "License plate detectives" for one week. Ask them to record the various state licenses they see during the week on the notebook paper, ones starting with A next to A, and so on. At the end of one week compare lists. You may wish to graph the results.

3. State abbreviation hunt. Provide the students with copies of the U.S. map student activity page. Call out an abbreviation of a state. The student can hunt for the abbreviation on his or her map and name the state. Vary this activity by calling out an abbreviation and asking the student to locate the state and name the state North of it, and so on.

Where Is My State ?

1 Do the ditto.

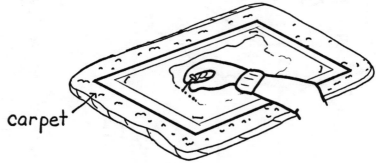

2 Make a state map pin design.

carpet

File Folder Directions

Where Is My State?

name _____

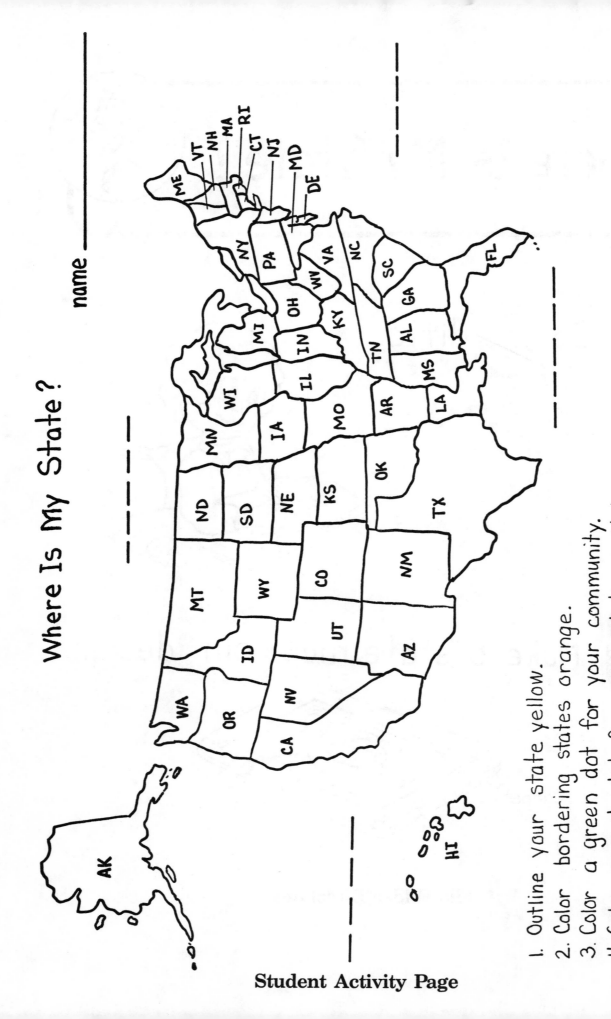

1. Outline your state yellow.
2. Color bordering states orange.
3. Color a green dot for your community.
4. Color a red dot for your state capital.
5. Color a state you would like to visit purple.
6. Color the oceans and lakes blue.

Student Activity Page

TEACHER'S DIRECTIONS FOR "MY STATE FLAG" CENTER

Content areas: Social studies, communication, motor

Skills: Using references, creating, creative writing, coordination

Materials needed:

> Copies of student activity page
> Teacher-made or commercial thermal transparency of state flag
> Overhead projector
> State flag
> Large white drawing paper
> Masking tape
> Pencil
> Scissors
> Crayons or water-base marking pens
> Staples and stapler
> Dowels, cardboard strips, or discarded wrapping paper rolls (one per student)
> References about your state flag such as encyclopedias, dictionaries, and booklets (State flag information booklets may be available from your secretary of state)
> **Optional:** teacher-made reference chart

Materials preparation:

1. Set up this center near a wall or chalkboard where an electrical outlet is available.
2. Provide a state flag.
3. Prepare a thermal transparency of your state flag to use on an overhead projector.
4. Show the students how to tape the paper onto the wall, use the transparency on the overhead projector to make the image of the flag, and trace the outline on the paper to create the state flag. Caution the students not to move the overhead projector while they are tracing.
5. **Optional:** you may want to use a copy of the student activity page to make a reference chart of flag information for younger students to copy.

DIRECTIONS FOR FILE FOLDER ACTIVITIES:

Activity 1

The student will draw the state flag as per your directions. Then he or she may color the flag the appropriate colors with crayons or marking pens, cut it out, and attach it to a dowel, cardboard strip, or roll.

Activity 2

The student writes about the state flag using references.

Thinking it over:

Discussion questions:

1. When was our state flag first used?
2. Has our state flag always been the same?
3. Who designed our flag?
4. Was a contest held for the best flag idea?
5. What do the colors on the flag represent?
6. Who made the first flag?
7. How did our school get a state flag?
8. Where can you buy state flags?
9. What flag rules do you know?

One step beyond activities:

1. Ask the students to observe and list the locations where state flags are flown in your community. Share the information in a class discussion about one week later.
2. Divide the class into small groups. Assign each group a list of specific states. They can find out information about the flags of the states, compare likenesses and differences, and draw pictures of the flags.
3. Creative writing. Some ideas are: "If I designed a new state flag . . . ," "If I could carry the state flag in a parade, I . . . ," "My state flag is special to me because . . ."

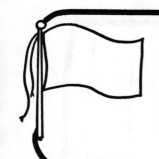 # My State Flag

1 Draw the
state flag.

2 Write about the flag.

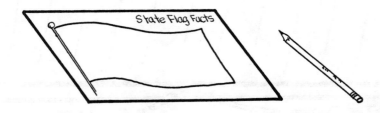

State Flag Facts

File Folder Directions

State Flag Facts

name

Student Activity Page

TEACHER'S DIRECTIONS FOR "MY STATE FLOWER" CENTER

Content areas: Social studies, communication, motor, science

Skills: Classifying, creative writing, creating, coordination, using references

Materials needed:

>   Paper
>   Copies of student activity page
>   A variety of art media such as tissue paper, fabric scraps, pipe cleaners, cotton, yarn, crepe paper, construction paper, foam scraps, fingerpaint, sponges, and so on
>   An assortment of crayons, marking pens, chalk, colored pencils
>   Glue
>   Pencil
>   Pictures of your state flower or a live plant
>   References: dictionary, pictionary, flower books such as Cox, Rosamund Kidman, and Cork, Barbara, *Usborne First Nature Flowers,* EDC Publishing, Tulsa, OK, 1980; Skelsey, Alice, and Huckaby, Gloria, *Growing Up Green,* Workman Publishing Co., New York, 1973; *National Geographic Picture Atlas of Our Fifty States,* National Geographic Society, Washington, D.C., 1978

Materials preparation:

1. You will need to determine the type of art media for your students to use in creating a likeness of your state flower.
2. You determine the kind of writing you want such as poetry, facts about your state flower, parts of the flower, and so on.

DIRECTIONS FOR FILE FOLDER ACTIVITIES:

Activity 1

The student makes the state flower as per your directions.

Activity 2

The student writes about the state flower on the student activity page as per your directions.

Thinking it over:

Discussion questions:

1. What is the name of our state flower?
2. How was the flower selected to become our state symbol?
3. Does every state have a flower as a symbol?
4. Is our state flower an endangered plant species?
5. Is there a fine for picking it?
6. Have you ever grown our state flower?
7. What conditions are needed for the best growth?

One step beyond activities:

1. Compare state flowers of different states. Younger students could fold paper into a 4 box format, write state names and draw state flowers in each box. Older students could use references for information about various state flowers such as name, growing conditions, climate, endangered species, and so on.
2. Invite a member of a local garden or conservation club to talk to your class about plants. Some topic ideas are: endangered plant species, do's and don'ts for picking flowers, location and importance of protected areas in your state (national and state forests, refuges, parks), how and where to grow state flowers, and conservation rules.

My State Flower

1 Make the State Flower.

2 Write about it.

File Folder Directions

My State Flower

_____

_____

_____

_____

_____

_____

_____

_____

_____

_____

_____

_____

_____

_____

_____

_____

_____

_____
name

Student Activity Page

TEACHER'S DIRECTIONS FOR "MY STATE TREE" PUZZLE CENTER

(Open-ended activity)

Content areas: Social studies, motor, teacher's choice, science

Skills: Classifying, creating, coordination, teacher's choice

Materials needed:

Copies of student activity page on heavy paper
Teacher-made reference chart
Pencil
Crayons
Scissors
One envelope per student (approximately $9\frac{1}{2}'' \times 4\frac{1}{4}''$)
Pictures of your state tree or book such as: Earle, Olive L., *State Trees* New York: William Morrow and Co., 1973; Sutton, Ann and Myron, *Audubon Society Nature Guides: Eastern Forests* New York: Alfred A. Knopf, 1985; Whitney, Stephen, *Audubon Society Nature Guides: Western Forests* New York: Alfred A. Knopf, 1985.

Materials preparation:

1. Establish background information about your state tree with pictures, books, or by observing a live one.
2. Determine a skill you wish to review or reinforce where answers could be arranged in sequence from lowest to highest. Some ideas are:

first	10 − 10 =	Write eight Spelling words in
second	15 − 14 =	alphabetical order (a–g, and so
third	12 − 10 =	on.)
fourth	17 − 14 =	
fifth	10 − 6 =	List eight state tree facts and
sixth	14 − 9 =	number them 1–8.
seventh	11 − 5 =	
eighth	13 − 6 =	

3. Make a reference chart of the skill.

DIRECTIONS FOR FILE FOLDER ACTIVITIES:

Activity 1

The student writes the information on the student activity page as per teacher's reference chart.

Then he or she turns over the student activity page and cuts the page on the *DASHED* lines.

Activity 2

The student draws the state tree on the back of the student activity page with crayons.

Then he or she turns over the student activity page and cuts the puzzle strips apart on the *SOLID* lines.

The student arranges the strips in sequential order. He or she turns the strips over one at a time thus forming a state tree puzzle. Then he or she can put the puzzle in an envelope labeled "My State Tree Puzzle" and his or her name.

Thinking it over:

Discussion questions:

1. What is the name of our state tree?
2. How was the tree selected to become our state symbol? When?
3. Does every state have a tree as a symbol?
4. Is our state tree deciduous or evergreen?
5. What changes occur in our tree during summer, fall, winter, and spring?
6. What are the parts of the tree?
7. What products are made from trees that grow in our state?

One step beyond activities:

1. Collect and press leaves from trees that grow in your state. The students can compare leaves and match them to pictures of the trees or names of the trees.
2. Visit a state tree in your area. The students can:
   a. Make leaf and bark rubbings.
   b. Predict the age of the tree.
   c. Listen to the tree with a stethoscope.
   d. Observe the tree at different times of the year and draw pictures of it. (You may prefer to take photographs.)
   e. List any animals or birds who visit the tree.

My State Tree Puzzle

1

1. Write on the strips.

2. Cut on the <u>dashed</u> lines.

2

Draw the state tree on the back.

Now cut on the <u>solid</u> lines.

File Folder Directions

Student Activity Page

TEACHER'S DIRECTIONS FOR "STATE WILDLIFE" CENTER

Content areas: Social studies, communication, motor, science

Skills: Using references, listening, creating

Materials needed:

> Paper
> Paint
> Paintbrushes
> Easel
> Cassette tape
> Tape recorder
> References: dictionary, pictionary, encyclopedias, books about your state wildlife

Materials preparation:

- You determine the kind of wildlife you want to have highlighted for this activity. Some ideas are animals, fish, or insects common to your state.
- Prepare a cassette tape of the book you have chosen.

DIRECTIONS FOR FILE FOLDER ACTIVITIES

Activity 1

The student listens to the cassette tape of the book.

Activity 2

The student paints a picture of the wildlife.

Optional activity:

The student can write about the wildlife using references.

Thinking it over:

Discussion questions:

1. What are some animals, fish, or insects that live in our state?
2. What are the regions of the state where they live?
3. Why do they live in our state?
4. Do any of the wildlife hibernate?
5. What wildlife have been designated as our state symbols?
6. How did they become official symbols? When?
7. Are any of the wildlife endangered species?
8. What is being done to protect them?
9. How can you help protect them?

One step beyond activities:

1. Conduct a class discussion about wildlife the students would like to have for state symbols. Make a class graph of their choices.
2. The students can write letters to your state lawmakers indicating the class choices for state symbols. (Contact your local library for information.) You may want to make this a whole school project. The students could make posters supporting different choices of wildlife and place them in hallways, and so on. Your students could poll the other classes for their choices, then write to the lawmakers.
3. Discuss the various kinds of wildlife that are endangered species. Some sources for background information are: Cadieux, Charles, *These Are the Endangered,* The Stone Wall Press, Inc., Washington, D.C., 1981 Audubon Society, 8940 Jones Mill Rd., Washington, D.C., 20015; Defenders of Wildlife, 1244 Nineteenth St. N.W., Washington, D.C., 20036 Izaak Walton League of America, Inc., 1800 N. Kent St., Suite 896, Arlington, VA., 22209; National Wildlife Federation, 1412 16th St., N.W., Washington, D.C.

State Wildlife

1 Listen to the book.

2 Paint the wildlife.

File Folder Directions

TEACHER'S DIRECTIONS FOR "MY STATE BIRD" CENTER

Content areas: Social studies, communication, motor, science

Skills: Classifying, comparing, creating, coordination, handwriting, using references

Materials needed:

> Handwriting paper
> Pencil
> Crayons
> Construction paper in assorted sizes and colors
> Scissors
> Paste
> Picture of your state bird
> Teacher-made state bird example
> Teacher-made bird reference chart
> References: a current almanac such as *The 1988 Information Please Almanac,* Houghton-Mifflin Co., Boston, 1987; Robbins, Chandler S., Brunn, Bertel, and Zim, Herbert S., *A Guide to Field Identification Birds of North America,* Golden Press, New York, 1983; Ross, Wilma, *Fabulous Facts about the 50 States,* Scholastic, Inc., New York, 1981.

Materials preparation.

1. Make an example of the state bird as pictured on the file folder directions.
   Materials needed:

   a. One 3″ × 8″ piece of construction paper the color of the body of your state bird.
   b. One 2″ × 6″ piece of construction paper the color of the head of your state bird.
   c. One 2″ × 6″ (or longer) piece of construction paper the color of the tail of your state bird.
   d. Small pieces of appropriately colored construction paper for the beak, feet, wings, and any additional parts, such as a crown.

How to construct the state bird:

   a. Form the paper strip for the body into a loop and paste the ends together.
   b. Form the paper strip for the head into a loop and paste the ends together.
   c. Paste the head loop onto the body loop.
   d. Fringe tail piece and paste it onto the body.
   e. Cut and paste the other additional parts onto the bird.

2. Make a bird reference chart as pictured on the file folder directions. Fold handwriting paper into three columns. Draw a small picture and write the name of your state bird in the first column. Draw two other state birds and write their names in the remaining two columns. (As of this writing the following birds are the state symbols for several states: Robin, Cardinal, Western Meadowlark, and Mocking Bird. Please consult a current almanac for up-to-date information.) If you are teaching younger students, you may want to list the states in each column which have the bird for their state symbol. Older students may use references to find out the required information.

DIRECTIONS FOR FILE FOLDER ACTIVITIES:

Activity 1

The student makes the state bird referring to your example.

Activity 2

The student folds the handwriting paper into three columns. He or she compares other state birds referring to your bird reference chart.

Optional Activity

The student may write a story about the state bird using appropriate references. Some ideas are: How and why was the state bird selected? What foods does it eat? What are its nesting habits? Does it migrate? (If so, where?)

Thinking it over:

Discussion questions:

1. What is the name of our state bird?
2. How was the bird chosen to become our state symbol? When?
3. What states have the same bird for their state symbol?
4. Does our state bird build a nest? Describe it.
5. What does the bird eat?
6. Does it migrate? Where? Why?
7. How many students feed the birds?
8. What kinds of food do you feed them?
9. What kinds of birds come to your yard?

One step beyond activities:

1. Discuss and trace migration routes of birds common to your area on the United States map. Determine what month the birds usually leave your area, where they will locate, when they will reach their destination, and predict the month they will return to your area. List birds who remain in your area year round.
2. Make a chart listing songs that have been written about your state bird. The students could be divided into small groups to research music books for the information. They could sing some of the songs familiar to them or learn new ones.
3. Encourage students to feed the birds. Discuss kinds of food. Make simple bird feeders. Two good books for references are: Cosgrove, Irene E., and Cosgrove Ed, *My Recipes Are for the Birds,* Doubleday and Co., Inc., Garden City, New York, 1975; Crook, Beverly Courtney, *Invite a Bird to Dinner,* Lothrop, Lee and Shepard Co., New York, 1978.

My State Bird

1 Make the State bird.

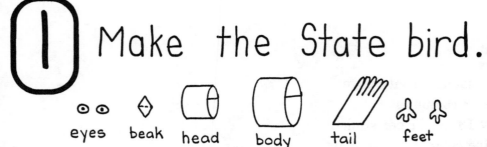

eyes beak head body tail feet

2

Compare other
State birds.

File Folder Directions

TEACHER'S DIRECTIONS FOR "STATE POTPOURRI" CENTER

Content areas: Social studies, communication, motor

Skills: Classifying, sorting, coordination, using references, spelling, vocabulary development

Materials needed:

> Copies of student activity page
> Typewriter or computer
> One 12″ by 18″ paper per student
> One 12″ pipe cleaner per student
> One plastic bag (approximately 12″ by 12″) per student
> Pencil
> Scissors
> Crayons
> A collection of 12 or more objects that are unique for your state such as products
> A container for the collection

Materials preparation:

1. Prepare a collection of objects or pictures of things that are unique for your state. Label each object. Put them into a container.
2. Instruct the students on the proper way to load the student activity page into the typewriter carriage. If this is the student's first experience with classroom typing, assure the students that mistakes will be acceptable. Encourage the students to proofread their typing *after* the paper is removed from the typewriter. They may use a pencil to cross out any errors or write in missing letters (no erasing is allowed).
3. If a typewriter is not available, these options may work:
(a) write the words on the student activity page (b) use a stamp letter set and ink pad to print the letters (c) use a computer and printer if the students have adequate skills.

DIRECTIONS FOR FILE FOLDER ACTIVITIES:

Activity 1

The student chooses eight objects from the collection. Then he or she folds paper into an eight box format. The student draws, colors, and writes the name of each of the eight objects on the paper. Then he or she cuts the paper apart on the folded lines.

Activity 2

The student types the names of the objects on the student activity page. He or she puts the eight paper objects into a bag. Then he or she cuts out the label on the student activity page and ties it onto the bag with a pipe cleaner.

Optional activity:

The older student may write information on the back of the paper objects such as areas of the state where the objects are found.

Thinking it over:

Discussion questions:

1. What crops are grown in our state?
2. What products are made from these crops?
3. What factories do we have in our area?
4. What do the factories manufacture?
5. What minerals are found in our state?
6. What are the uses of the minerals?
7. Does our state have oil or gas?
8. Does our state have forests?
9. Are trees being cut from these forests?
10. What products are made from these trees?

One step beyond activities:

1. The students could write letters to people they know in other states. They could send their State Potpourri Bags to them.
2. Make charts of things unique to your state. Divide the class into small groups. Assign each group a different category, such as crops, food products, manufactured products, minerals, or other natural resources. Provide references for the students. The students may draw pictures or cut them out of magazines, catalogs, and newspapers to paste onto their charts.

 This
'n
That!

State Potpourri

1 Choose 8 things.

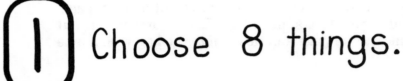

Draw them.   Cut them out.

2

Type a label
for the bag.

Now cut it out.
Tie it on the bag.

File Folder Directions

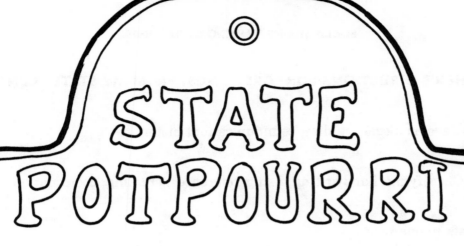

STATE POTPOURRI

This bag contains unique things from my state.

Ingredients:

_____
my name

Student Activity Page

TEACHER'S DIRECTIONS FOR "GREETINGS! FROM MY STATE" CENTER

Content areas: Social studies, communication, motor

Skills: Classifying, handwriting, using references, creating, coordination

Materials needed:

>   Copies of student activity pages
>   One piece of 12″ by 18″ oaktag per student
>   Crayons
>   Pencil
>   Scissors
>   Masking tape
>   One envelope per student (approximately 4″ by 5″)
>   References: books about your state, dictionary, pictionary
>   Teacher-made post card reference strip

Materials preparation:

Make an example strip of post cards as pictured on the file folder directions:

1. Fold and cut a 12″ by 18″ piece of oaktag in half lengthwise.
2. Fold each 6″ by 9″ oaktag strip into fourths.
3. Join the two strips together with masking tape.
4. Write or draw pictures of any information your students may need on the post cards on the student activity pages.
5. Cut out the post cards and paste them onto the front side of the oaktag strip in numerical order.
6. You determine an assignment for your students to complete on the back side of the post card strip. Older students could use references to write information describing the person, building, symbol, and so on featured on the front of the cards. Younger students could copy any written information you provide on the reference strip. You may want the students to draw eight pictures of places they have visited in your state.

DIRECTIONS FOR FILE FOLDER ACTIVITIES:

Activity 1

The student makes the post cards as per teacher directions.

Activity 2

The student makes the oaktag strip as per teacher directions. The student pastes the postcards in numerical order onto the strip. He or she completes the back side of the strip as per teacher directions. The student puts the strip into an envelope.

Thinking it over:

Discussion questions:

1. Who is the governor of our state?
2. What does the governor do?
3. Where does the governor work?
4. Where is the Capitol Building located?
5. Who works in the Capitol Building?
6. What is our state motto?
7. What is the meaning of the state motto?
8. What famous park is in our state?
9. Does our state have a stone for a symbol?
10. What stones are found in our state?
11. What famous people are from our state?
12. Does our state have an animal for a symbol?
13. What animals live in our state?

One step beyond activities:

1. Encourage students to share their post cards with the other students in your class or other classes. Suggest that the students mail their post cards in an envelope to someone who lives in another state.
2. Ask the students to bring their post cards they have received from other people. They also may bring post cards they have collected on trips. The students can attach the cards with yarn and map pins to the appropriate locations on the United States map.

Greetings! From My State

1 Make the post cards.

2 Paste the post cards.

tape

Paste

File Folder Directions

1. My State

2. State Capitol Building

3. The Governor

4. State Motto

Student Activity Page

5. A Famous Park

6. A Stone from My State

7. A Famous Person

8. An Animal from My State

Student Activity Page

TEACHER'S DIRECTIONS FOR "STATE" ENRICHMENT ACTIVITIES

"State" Group Activity

Celebrate Our State Day.

"State" Home Activity

Duplicate the pages on colored paper. Send the pages home one month prior to beginning the State Social Studies unit. This should give students ample time to obtain travel information.

"State" Awards

Duplicate the pages on colored paper. Give each child who returns the "State" Home Activity a Home Activity Award. The other State Awards may be used for the recognition of good work, and so on.

"State" Summary Activity

Duplicate the "State" Summary pages on heavy paper. The students may review the state information, illustrate and cut out the labeled shapes. On the reverse side of the shapes, the students write clever riddles about the symbols. On Celebrate Our State Day, divide the students into small groups to share their riddles. The students may make state displays as shown. As an extended activity, you also may wish to submit selected riddles to the newspaper or local radio station to publicize Celebrate Our State Day.

"STATE" GROUP ACTIVITIES

As a culminating event for the State Social Studies unit, hold a "Celebrate Our State Day."

Plan many activities including sharing the "Great Getaway" state adventures, and constructing the state mobiles.

Other ideas are:

1. Plant a state tree or flowers on your school property. Sources to obtain these plants:

    a. The students could hold appropriate fund raisers to generate monies for the purchases.
    b. The students could contact local nurseries for possible donations.
    c. The students could contact your state department of natural resources for help.

2. The students could write your state governor six to eight months prior to the Celebrate Our State Day.

    a. Send a newsletter describing the Celebrate Our State events.
    b. Invite the governor to attend the events. (The mayor or city administrators may be used as backup choices.)
    c. Ask him or her for free state tourism advertising items.
    d. Ask for help in obtaining a state flag for your classroom or school.

3. Play State Symbol Bingo: The students will need to fold a 9" × 12" paper into a 16-box format. Then copy 16 words in random order from the chalkboard (include your state symbols and some non-symbols) onto the paper. You or a designated student call the 16 words, the students cover the state symbol names with paper markers. The winner needs to cover four words in a row or four corners. The winner may be the caller for the next game.

4. Plan a grade level or whole school assembly with different classes sharing their state projects. You also may want to have a parade featuring student-made flags.

"STATE" HOME ACTIVITY
ENRICHMENT PAGE

RETURN BY _____

Date _____

Dear Parent,

On _____ we will have a "Celebrate Our State" day at school to culminate our state social studies unit.

One of the events of the day will give students an opportunity to share "Great Getaway" state adventures.

Please help your child plan a trip from your home to another area of our state by land transportation. You may encourage your child to obtain travel information (brochures, post cards, tourism information, and so on) from chambers of commerce, travel bureaus, and state tourism offices.

On _____ he or she will need to bring one suitcase (or similar luggage) containing:

1. "_____'s Great Getaway Plans"
   your child

2. A state map with the round trip route highlighted with marking pen.

3. One outfit of clothing for the trip.

4. A maximum of 10 additional trip items.

Please encourage your child to keep his or her "Great Getaway" plans a secret to prevent duplication of trips.

Thank you for your help with this special project.

Sincerely,

Your child's teacher

"_____'s Great Getaway Plans"

your name

Date of departure _____

Date of return _____

People who will travel with me _____

_____

Destination area _____

Places to stay overnight _____

_____

_____

Mode of travel _____

Round trip mileage _____

Trip allowance _____

Special places to visit 1. _____

2. _____

3. _____

4. _____

List any additional plans on the back of this paper.
PACK THIS IN YOUR SUITCASE AND RETURN ON _____

Let's Go!

I've completed the
Home Activity.
I'm ready to go to:

_____

_____
name

Home Activity Award

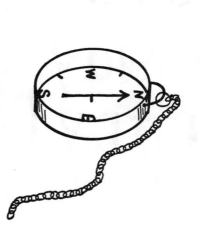

From north to south
And east to west,
I sure know why
My State is best !

_____
name

State Award

I'm **wild** about your work!

Flying High!

Love the way you try!

State Awards

State Tree

State Bird

State Flag

State Flower

State
Capital

Summary

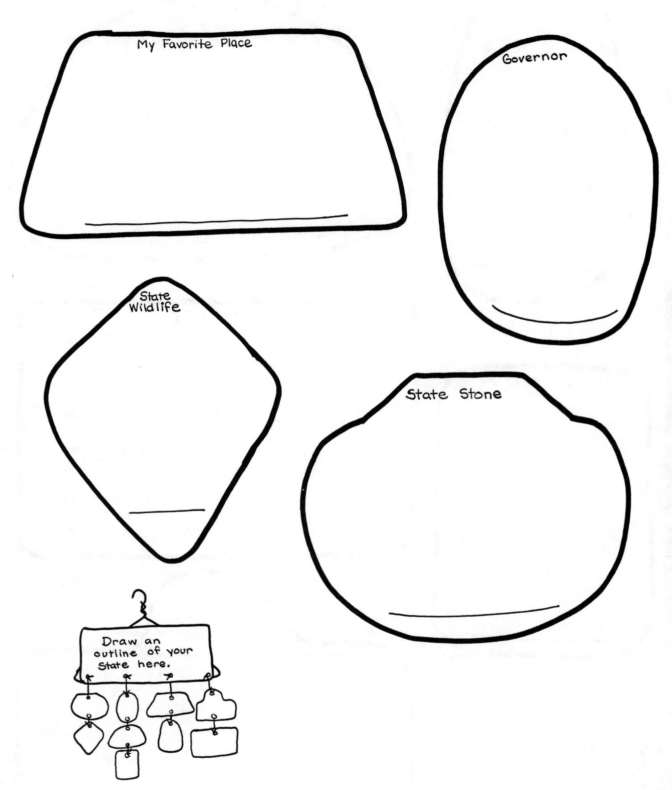

My Favorite Place

Governor

State Wildlife

State Stone

Draw an outline of your State here.

Make a display about your State.

Summary

LEARNING CENTER MANAGEMENT

If you are using Learning Centers now, you have already developed a method to manage them.

If you want to begin using Learning Centers, but need management techniques, you may want to try a management system which has worked successfully for us. A brief synopsis of this system is given in this chapter. More specific details of this system are described extensively in the following book: Poppe, Carol A., and Van Matre, Nancy A., *Science Learning Centers for the Primary Grades*. The Center for Applied Research in Education, Inc., West Nyack, New York 1985.

Additional Learning Center ideas are given in the book Poppe, Carol A., and Van Matre, Nancy A., *K-3 Science Activities Kit*. The Center for Applied Research in Education, Inc., West Nyack, New York 1988.

HOW TO MANAGE A LEARNING CENTER SYSTEM

This system features Learning Center Unit activities as an integral part of a daily schedule.

The children are taught in a traditional manner for the initial three weeks of the school year. All of the children are assigned morning Seatwork. You work with small groups of children to assess their Reading ability.

You establish four Reading groups based on ability. Each group is given a color name: red, yellow, orange, and green.

After the four groups are established the children are introduced to a new morning routine. (See the sample Morning Schedule.)

The children move every one half hour to four areas of the classroom to do Seatwork, Boardwork, Reading, and Learning Center activities (one child per Learning Center).

A Color Wheel displayed near the Reading area aids in the clockwise movement of the four groups to the four areas of the room.

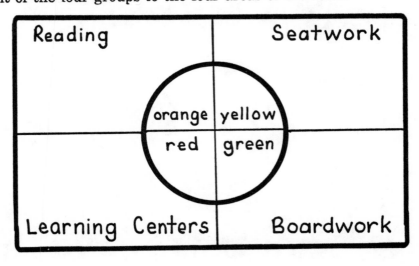

You turn the Color Wheel clockwise after you have completed one half hour with a Reading group. The groups rotate until they have completed the four areas (approximately two hours every morning).

A "Make-up" time of approximately fifteen minutes is held after all four Reading groups are finished. Children with incomplete work (which has been placed in a box labeled "Make-up") have the opportunity to complete their work. The other children use this time for games, books, etc.

The afternoon schedule consists of whole group activities: Math, Writing, Gym, Science, Art, and so on.

MORNING SCHEDULE

Rotation diagrams (circular charts):

Diagram 1 — Reading / Seatwork / Boardwork / Learning Centers; colors: orange, yellow, red, green

Diagram 2 — Reading / Seatwork / Boardwork / Learning Centers; colors: red, orange, green, yellow

Diagram 3 — Reading / Seatwork / Boardwork / Learning Centers; colors: green, red, yellow, orange

GROUP	9:00–9:30	9:30–10:00	10:00–10:15	10:15–10:45	10:45–11:15	11:15–11:30
Orange	Reading	Seatwork	Recess	Boardwork	Learning centers	Makeup
Yellow	Seatwork	Boardwork	Recess	Learning centers	Reading	Makeup
Red	Learning centers	Reading	Recess	Seatwork	Boardwork	Makeup
Green	Boardwork	Learning centers	Recess	Reading	Seatwork	Makeup

8:30–9:00: Whole class is at seatwork and boardwork desks for opening and seatwork, boardwork directions.

HOW TO SET UP THE CLASSROOM INTO FOUR AREAS (SEATWORK, BOARDWORK, READING, AND LEARNING CENTERS)

The arrangement of the furniture in the classroom is important in creating a good learning environment. The room should be set up to give the students the freedom to move physically and academically from one area to another.

Prior to the first day of school arrange the furniture to create four areas: Seatwork, Boardwork, Reading, and Learning Centers. It is easier to develop a set routine in the beginning weeks of the school year, than to rearrange the classroom when you start the four group movement (approximately a month later).

The main area of the classroom should be divided into two parts for Seatwork and Boardwork. Bookcases, storage boxes, and so on, can be placed in a long row to serve as a main divider between the Seatwork and Boardwork areas.

The desks in the Boardwork area will usually face a chalkboard. The students will be copying your assignments from the chalkboard. Some ideas are: poems, riddles, creative writing, facts, vocabulary lists, etc. related to the theme of the Social Studies Unit.

In the Seatwork area, the desks do not need to face the chalkboard. Seatwork activities may include: Phonics, Mathematics, Science, Spelling, Social Studies, and Reading ditto or workbook pages.

HOW TO ASSIGN DESKS

An important factor to consider in room arrangement is the assignment of desks. Each child can have a permanently assigned desk to use before school and during the whole-group activities of the day. In order to accommodate the mobility of the four groups to seatwork, boardwork, learning centers, and reading, all of the desk tops can be shared by everyone. (You may need to establish a rule that everyone works on desk tops only.)

There is an alternative method for seating that allows for maximum mobility in the classroom. The children do not have any assigned desks, only the tops of the desks are used, not the insides. You may prefer to turn the desks so the open ends are away from the seated children.

Each student needs to have a box for pencils, crayons, scissors, and paste to use at the four work areas of the room. The box may be stored in his or her desk or on a bookshelf.

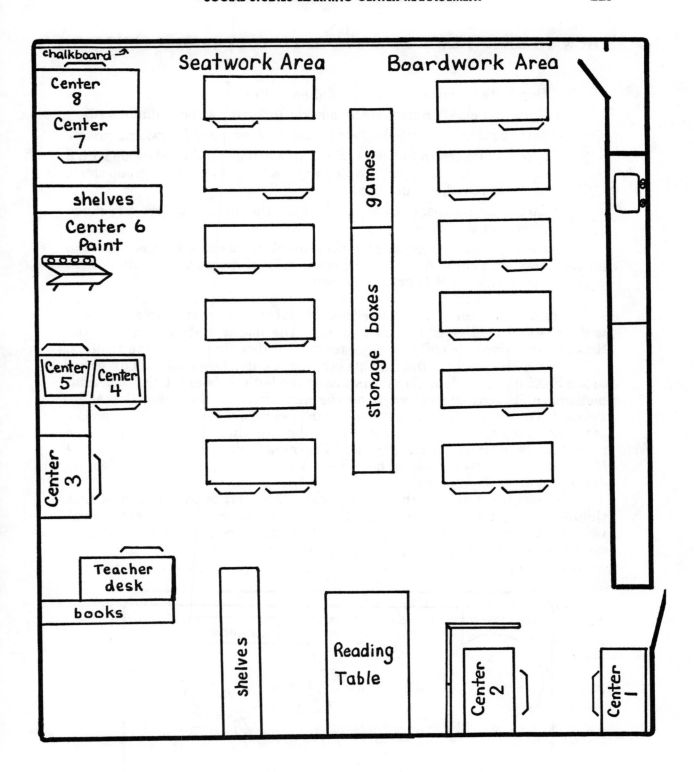

HOW TO KEEP TRACK OF EACH CHILD AT LEARNING CENTERS

- Duplicate a marker for each child as pictured.
- Write the child's name on the marker (*after* it has been duplicated).
- Sort the markers into the four groups (red, orange, yellow, and green).
- Circle a different number on each child's marker in the red group with a permanent marking pen. (In this way, each child in the red group starts at a different Learning Center.)
- Circle the numbers on the markers for the orange, yellow, and green groups in the same way.
- Pass out the markers to each child to color and cut out. (It is helpful to have each child color his marker the color of his group, especially with the initial set of Learning Centers.)

After the children have colored and cut out their markers staple them on a bulletin board or divider into four groups. The markers should be near the Reading area since the children move there after they finish Learning Centers.

When the child has finished his Learning Center, he moves with his group to the Reading area. He finds his marker on the bulletin board. Using a permanent marking pen, he puts an X on the number of the Learning Center he finished. Then he circles the next number in clockwise order. This is the number of the Learning Center where he will work the following day. He continues this pattern daily until he has completed all Learning Centers (one per day). In the Mirror example pictured below, he would do a total of eight Learning Centers during an eight day period.

If a child is absent, the teacher marks Ab. next to the number of that child's Learning Center. Then the teacher circles the following day's center number. The Learning Centers missed due to absences are *not* made up. This is essential in keeping one child per Learning Center.

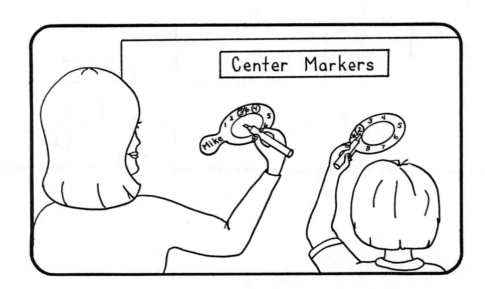

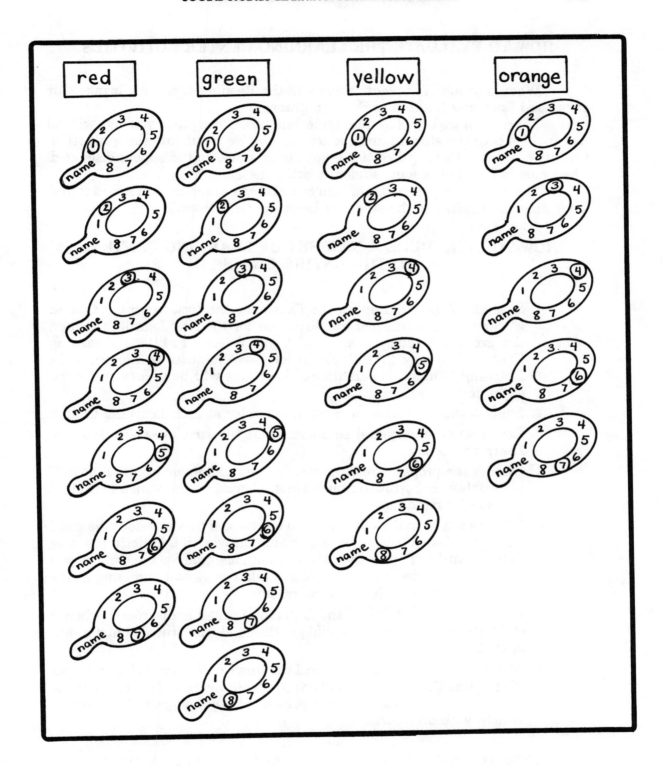

HOW TO EVALUATE THE LEARNING CENTER ACTIVITIES

When a group of students rotates to the Reading area they bring their completed Learning Centers work to be graded.

There are a variety of evaluation techniques. One method you may wish to use enables both the student and the teacher to give input into the evaluation. Quality of work, following directions, ways to improve, and so on, are discussed. The grade is based on a joint student-teacher decision.

The enrichment activities of each Social studies unit contain award forms. They may be attached to the student's Learning Center work.

HOW TO INTRODUCE A NEW SET OF LEARNING CENTERS TO THE ENTIRE CLASS

1. Seat all of the children on the floor near the first Learning Center. (After you have finished the directions for the first Learning Center, the group continues to move with you to each additional Learning Center. This may take thirty to forty-five minutes to explain eight Learning Centers. No additional directions will be necessary for the eight day period.)

2. Explain the directions in consecutive order at each Learning Center.

3. Demonstrate any special equipment (e.g. filmstrip pre-viewer) at the Learning Center.

4. Discuss the proper care of materials (e.g. mirrors or fragile items). If materials were borrowed from a Media Center, you may wish to emphasize special handling.

5. Indicate any activities that need to be checked by you before the child leaves the Learning Center (e.g. manipulatives on a bulletin board or flannelboard or floor activities). Work out a signal for the child so you don't forget to check his work (e.g. Child can remain standing at the Learning Center with two arms raised).

6. Discuss clean-up rules. If the Learning Center is disorderly when a child goes to it, he or she should get the child who preceded him or her to clean up.

7. Allow time for questions at each Learning Center. By explaining a set of Learning Centers thoroughly, you will eliminate daily interruptions. A child may quietly ask another person in his or her group for additional help with directions.

HOW TO EXPLAIN LEARNING CENTERS TO PARENTS

The following letter is sent home on the first day that Learning Centers are used (approximately the third week of September).

ALL ABOUT LEARNING CENTERS

Date _____

Dear Parent:

During the first few weeks of school, I have been reviewing the skills your child has learned in the past. The children have been given a variety of tests. I wanted to find out where each child was regarding these skillls and take him or her from that point on.

Today we began a new morning routine which we will follow all year. The children have been divided into four groups based on reading ability. The four groups are: red, green, yellow, and orange. The children move every one half hour to four areas of the classroom to do Seatwork, Boardwork, Reading, and Learning Center activities.

A Color Wheel (in the center of this diagram) helps all of us keep track of where we are working:

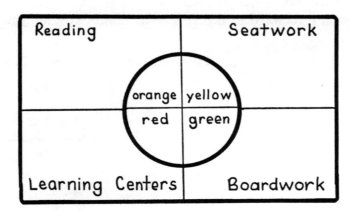

In this diagram, the orange group is working with me at the Reading area, the yellow group is doing Seatwork (Math and Phonics papers), the green group is at the Boardwork area (copying some type of work from the chalkboard), and the red group is working at eight different Learning Centers (one child per Learning Center). At the end of one half hour, the Color Wheel is turned clockwise and all of the groups move to the next area. The groups continue to move this way until each group has completed all four areas.

A make-up time is given after the children have completed all four areas. This enables all of the children to finish their morning work.

In the afternoon we have whole group activities: Math, Science, Art, Social Studies, Handwriting, Spelling, and so on.

There are several reasons why I am teaching with Learning Centers: (1.) The classroom is quieter to teach reading. (2.) A structured routine is followed daily. (3.) The children learn to follow directions. (4.) Independent study habits are established. (5.) The children can pace themselves to work for thirty minutes. (6.) The children learn to evaluate themselves. (7.) A wide variety of subjects provide experiences in learning something new, reinforcing old skills, or developing creativity.

The opportunity to participate in Learning Centers will be a new experience for many of our children. The beginning days of Learning Centers may present many new adjustments. We will have a routine established within a week.

Our Social Studies Learning Centers will focus on a child's awareness of himself and his environment. I have prepared activities for eight individual Learning Centers covering the following skills: Mapping, Math, Art, Social Studies, Reading, Listening, Handwriting, and Coordination.

During the next eight school days the Learning Centers will be based on the theme _____. If you have books, records, games, and so on, about these Learning Centers, please send them.

You are welcome to visit us any morning to see our Learning Centers in action. I am looking forward to meeting you. Thank you for your support.

Sincerely,

_____

Your child's teacher